This book is packed with real-life insights for powerful ministry, based on biblical principles and field experience. It is well worth reading and pondering.

—C. Peter Wagner, Presiding Apostle
International Coalition of Apostles

In *Ruling in the Gates*, Joseph Mattera presents a challenge to the "me-centered" focus in many of today's churches and ministries. This book is a call to the church to understand her purpose on earth and fully engage society to fulfill the biblical mission. Through years of experience and research, Mattera has found the key to unlocking closed and misinforming paradigms regarding the role of the church in the earth today.

—Apostle John P. Kelly, President and Founder LEAD
(Leadership Education for Apostolic Development)
Ambassador Apostle, ICA
(International Coalition of Apostles)

Joseph Mattera is one of the emerging voices calling the church to relevance, biblical standards and societal leadership. With the heart and common sense of a local church pastor, and the breadth and vision of a citywide leader, Joe encourages all of us in this vital book to let our walk with Christ mov _apostle the walk of the chur_ ch and effectively impact ou  l be dangerous to apathy!

D1125201

:v. Robert Stearns
Wings Ministries
New York, NY

Fresh voices are calling for a new Reformation, first of the church and then of society. This time they speak, not the Latin of the European monasteries and universities, but the vernacular accents of the Urban Third World. That is where the Spirit of God is moving the most, where the church is not only growing, but actually contending for the Lordship of Christ. Joseph Mattera, a gifted urban church leader from Brooklyn, lifts his voice with urgency. He hits upon the myths and weaknesses of the church, calling with holy impatience for God's kingdom to come, and for His will to be done on earth. This book will make you uncomfortable; resist the urge to dismiss it by hairsplitting the theology or excusing your complacency behind "the blessed hope." Get used to the new, urban rhythm of the Church Militant, and if you can, get in step with our multi-ethnic brethren. They are leading the way towards our coming King.

—JOSE L. GONZALEZ
PRESIDENT, SEMILLA
ADJUNCT INSTRUCTOR, REGENT UNIVERSITY

In *Ruling in the Gates*, Joseph Mattera passionately communicates God's concern for the Christian church to become culturally aware, socially relevant, and kingdom minded. As a skilled litigator of biblical truth, he presents and defends the case for citywide unity among the clergy while exposing the inherent weakness in rugged individualism. The reader will take away strength and clarity in how to integrate with other believers to demonstrate the gospel of the kingdom of God.

—DAVID D. IRELAND, PH.D.
SENIOR PASTOR, CHRIST CHURCH,
MONTCLAIR, NJ

"Seek ye first the Kingdom and everything else will be added to you." However, many times we get stopped in how to seek and stay focused to win the battle at our next gate of influence. Joseph Mattera captures the mission and purpose of Jesus in *Ruling in the Gates*. Through this book he also transfers that "christos" anointing of Jesus to the Lord's church leadership today. God is establishing an apostolic/prophetic leadership for the future harvest of the church. This book releases "strength to turn the battle at your gate."

—DR. CHUCK D. PIERCE
VICE PRESIDENT, GLOBAL HARVEST MINISTRIES
PRESIDENT, GLORY OF ZION INTERNATIONAL MINISTRIES, INC.

It is true that revelation leads to revolution. How we see directs our actions. In *Ruling in the Gates*, Dr. Joseph

Mattera does exactly that; he is placing his hands around our faces and turning our heads to understand our community and calling from a biblical worldview. This book is not written to inform; it is written to incite a revolution! Dr. Mattera is a dangerous man with the revelatory word. You will not quote from this book; your lifestyle, after reading this book, will become a personified quote—it will be you.

—Dr. Samuel R. Chand, D.D.
President, Beulah Heights Bible College,
Atlanta, Georgia

Joe Mattera has written a far-reaching survey of the relationship between God's kingdom, the church, and their relationship to both one another and society. It is filled with insight, practical observation and the kind of biblical analysis that will stir men's passions. It is certainly "cutting edge," yet reaches back into church history for theological precedence. It is not just another "feel good" Christian book; its implications cannot help but lead serious readers into the kind of crisis from which people and nations change.

—Dennis Peacocke
President and Founder, Strategic Christian Services
Santa Rose, California

Pastor Joe Mattera is addressing a tremendously important issue for the twenty-first century church—understanding the reign of God's kingdom in all of its dimensions through His church. He has an important sense of God's vision for a united church transforming cities in every sphere.

—Dr. McKenzie (Mac) Pier
President, Concerts of Prayer, Greater New York

Dr. Joseph Mattera has outdone himself! This is a brilliant book that will not only inspire but fill believers with practical revelation that will enable them to effectively fulfill their roles in society.

—Lenny Weston
Vision Ministries International

Joe Mattera speaks prophetically to a religious world reeling between utopian theologies and failing ideologies with a message of hope and triumph. Prepare to be challenged. This book calls Christians to their biblical role to train and empower the church to be nation changers in every area of society.

—BOB PHILLIPS
SENIOR PASTOR, ENCOURAGER CHURCH
HOUSTON, TEXAS

Ruling in the Gates is an outstanding and thoroughly thought-out book with irresistible persuasions for the church in the city to rise up and be victorious in these crucial times. I highly recommend this book to anyone who is serious about being a part of leading edge Christianity in this third millennium.

—PASTOR JEFF BEACHAM
FIREPOWER MINISTRIES INTERNATIONAL

An armchair philosopher Joe Mattera is not. To consider the scriptures, concepts and revelation he has presented, is to understand the heart of a man in the urban trenches. He has not allowed time or battles to dim his vision, nor has he capitulated to the negativism and doubt of many who view the city. Rather, he is full of faith and vision, convinced that the "kingdoms of this world are becoming the kingdoms of our Lord and of His church." Because revelation is progressive, these foundational truths will soon be manifested, bringing glory unto Him in the church both now and forever.

—REV. ROBERT JOHANSSON, SR.
PASTOR, EVANGEL CHURCH
QUEENS, NY

Rarely have I come across such a passion for the church and the city as the one that dominates this book from the opening sentence to the final paragraph. A must-read for every pastor and lay church leader!

—FRIEDHELM K. RADANDT
PRESIDENT EMERITUS
THE KING'S COLLEGE

RULING IN THE GATES

JOSEPH MATTERA

CREATION
HOUSE PRESS®

RULING IN THE GATES by Joseph Mattera
Published by Creation House Press
A part of Strang Communications Company
600 Rinehart Road
Lake Mary, Florida 32746
www.creationhouse.com

Unless otherwise noted, all Scripture quotations are from the King James Version of the Bible.

Scripture quotations marked NIV are from the Holy Bible, New International Version. Copyright © 1973, 1978, 1984, International Bible Society. Used by permission.

Cover design by Karen Gonzalves
Interior design by David Bilby

Library of Congress Catalog Card Number: 2003103160
International Standard Book Number: 1-59185-222-6

03 04 05 06 — 8 7 6 5 4 3 2 1
Printed in the United States of America.

I dedicate this book to the Lordship of Jesus Christ
over all of creation, and to the past, present
and future reformers who are partnering
with Him to make this a reality.

FOREWORD

The winds of change are blowing powerfully through the church today. After walking with Christ for thirty-one years, I can say we are being blown back on course again.

God gave me a word several years ago that the church was way off course and it was time for a major course correction. I have spent most of my life around the water. From surfing to fishing, I love being on or in the water, especially the ocean. As an avid waterman, I have studied the art of navigation. When you start off on a trip across the ocean for example, there are many elements to contend with to reach your predetermined destination. There is the boat itself, the wind, the currents, the waves and the weather—especially storms—that have to be worked with in order to stay on course. But the church has tried to avoid the storms, only to be swept along by the currents (traditions and fads) in order to seek easier sailing at the cost of getting way off course.

The emergence of the apostolic, Christocentric church living out the commission of Christ through passionate displays of first century New Testament reality in the twenty-first century is awesome. The words and actions of the *new* church are full of life and change. The idea of one church working together in a city, as well as the idea of this church moving in and through every arena of society is the biggest course correction to come to the church in America in a hundred years. The church of the twenty-first century has the opportunity to bring about the greatest reformation that has ever been witnessed.

The book you are about to read is a clear fact that this new move, this heavenly course correction, is well under way. Dr. Mattera, whom I have known for the past ten years, has stepped to the helm to bring a turn—a model—for all of us to use to bring about God's plan for this next great course change. I don't think it will be easy. Turning a ship into the storm where all the currents (trends, traditions), the waves (of doctrines of man) and the winds (adversity, resistance) will test even the sturdiest of ships.

I have been on the open water when storms come and the best place is to turn straight into the storm and stay on course. Because when the storm lifts, and it will, your city will be right on course for the greatest outpouring of God we have ever seen.

If you are tired of drifting along in passive, calm, safe water, while moving further and further from God's destiny for you and your city, then *Ruling in the Gates* is the right navigational chart for you to plot a fresh new course towards God's kingdom being established in your city. Tighten your sails, and begin changing your course!

—BISHOP BART PIERCE
A FELLOW CITY TAKER

CONTENTS

Introduction: The Gospel of the Kingdom . . . . *xiii*

1 The Birth of the Prayer Movement 1

2 The Mission of the Church 3

3 The Purpose of the Cross. 5

4 The Gospel of the Kingdom or the
   Gospel of American Culture. 7

5 The Kingdom of God. 11

6 The Real Reason They Crucified Jesus 15

7 The Nature of the Church
   and the Grand Commission 17

8 Are You Looking for Antichrist
   or for the Victorious Christ?. 21

9 Do You Have a Platonic Relationship
   With God and the World? 27

10 The Next Move: Incarnation 29

11 Are You Living in a Ghetto?. 33

12 The Coming Apostolic Reformation 47

13 Ten Things About the
   Gospel of the Kingdom. 55

14 The Consequences of the Kingdom. 83

15 Common Misconceptions Clarified. 87

   Epilogue. 91

   Notes 93

   Recommended Reading 95

THE GOSPEL OF THE KINGDOM

I write this book out of my understanding of apostolic* ministry and the gospel of the kingdom. My life's message is the lordship of Jesus Christ. In 1991 I started initiating citywide prayer events called All-City Prayer, which have had as many as sixty churches and over two thousand people praying for revival. From these prayer meetings I have seen covenant relationships develop among pastors and spiritual leaders in our city, which have resulted in the following:

- Monthly ministers' prayer meetings
- Pastors' support group
- Pastors' wives fellowship
- Community development strategies
- Evangelism strategies
- Urban Commission (short-term mission teams in New York)
- Unity Communion Services (uniting pastors across racial and denominational lines for the purpose of making covenant together)
- The Lighthouses of Prayer movement
- Operation Unity (apostolic fathers from every borough of New York joining together to reach our city)
- New York City Intercessors (intercessors released by their pastors to come together corporately to cover our city in intercession)
- City Covenant Coalition (an urban apostolic network based in the New York City region)

Pastors and ministries from our network of churches in South Brooklyn have gone on to be a part of major moves of God beyond our local area. One pastor joined the national leadership of Promise Keepers in their racial reconciliation component; another pastor directs the New York City March for Jesus. In addition to directing City Covenant Coalition, I also serve as one of the trustees of Concert of Prayer Greater New York that gives leadership to the prayer movement in Metropolitan New York area.

Many leaders claim that what we are doing is one of the most developed networking of autonomous churches in any big city in the country. Not only has the impact of this cooperation affected the churches in New York City, but also it has been documented that crime in our city has dropped dramatically since 1993.[1] We give God all the praise and glory.

When people ask me if I pastor an independent or a denominational church, I say neither. When they look at me with confusion and consternation, I tell them that I am a part of an interdependent church that is part of the church of New York City.

All of these experiences have greatly changed my paradigm as to how the church should be identified and how it should function in a city. They have also opened my eyes as to the purpose of the gospel. In the following pages you will see the ideas that I now espouse.

What you will be reading will not be new revelation, but I believe it will only be a recapitulation of the beliefs of the apostles, apostolic fathers and the great reformers. If I am the only one presently saying what is written in this book, or if it is a "new revelation" without roots in the historic church—then I will be the first to admit that it is heretical.

In this book I contend that in this postmodern post-Christian society and culture, western culture is way past the need for revival. What we need is a heaven-sent reformation that can serve as the underpinning and foundation of a revival. This is the missing link in terms of what must first happen in the church and in society. Revival is not enough, because we have fallen away from the biblical world view as the standard of law for our nation.

This can explain why most revivals in North America are short-lived in terms of their duration and cultural impact (if there was any impact at all!). We can no longer only look to Whitefield, Wesley and Finney as our models for revival, because during their time there was already in place a strong Christian worldview in terms of what our nation accepted as its mores.

Consequently, the effects of the First Great Awakening lasted generations and was most likely the impetus for the War for Independence from England.

The effects of the Second Great Awakening also lasted generations and resulted in many societal reforms including the Abolitionist (antislavery) Movement.

Nowadays, those affected by our church revivals fail to impact their surroundings, because the cultural underpinnings that underlie their places of employment base their values, methodology and purpose on secular humanism. This pressures the average Christian's views about life and God to remain relegated to the church community, thus continuing to separate the spiritual aspect of their faith from the biblical application to the natural world.

Revival and awakening bring people into the Church—reformation places both godly saints and systems into every facet of culture.

I pray that this book, which is primarily a prophetic apologetic for wholistic, apostolic* ministry, will be a catalyst to help move you into the full potential you have as part of the Church of the Lord Jesus Christ.

---

*There is some confusion as to the meaning of the terms *apostle* and *apostolic*. Without getting into an exhaustive explanation, when I use the word *apostle*, I am generally referring to a person who functions (with or without the title) in the first of the five ministry gifts listed in Ephesians 4:11 (i.e., apostles, prophets, evangelists, pastors and teachers). Some of the common attributes of contemporary apostles are as follows:

- They pastor a church or head up a ministry or corporation with regional, national or international influence that reaches beyond their local community.

- They are leaders of other leaders (or a pastor to other pastors).

- They are involved in the raising up or the multiplication of leadership.

- They have an entrepreneurial spirit and are capable of replicating themselves through the development of other ministers and ministries.

This book posits that there are apostles, as well as all of the other *fivefold* ministry gifts that God raises up specifically to reach into every area of society under His kingdom rule.

I use the term *apostolic* as an adjective, related to that same ministry gift function, describing a confluence of networks, church associations, ministries, businesses and other institutions and enterprises that function under God's rule.

CHAPTER 1

THE BIRTH OF THE PRAYER MOVEMENT

Since John Dawson's groundbreaking book at the end of the 1980s *Taking Our Cities for God*,[1] there has been an acceleration of the body of Christ in strategic spiritual warfare and in prayer. Since then men like George Otis Jr. and others have taught us about spiritual mapping and prayer walking. David Bryant and Concerts of Prayer have called us together to pray for revival, and Mike Bickle brought us the *Houses of Prayer* concept. The result is that there is more united, purposeful and strategic prayer going on right now than perhaps in the history of the nation.

Instead of individual saints and churches praying in a discursive way, haphazardly flinging "Scud missiles," the body of Christ is now praying "smart bombs" in a concerted effort that is shaking our cities.

Being an analytical person by nature, there was one area that dissatisfied me—even with all the smart bombs going forth I felt that in some major way we were still unfocused. Stephen Covey taught us in *The 7 Habits of Highly Effective People* to begin with the end in mind.[2] In other words, we will never be able to be effective in anything we do unless we first know why we are doing it and what our goals are. Your *eschatology* (what you believe about the future) determines your *teleology* (where you are going personally—your goals).

I have found that many people are praying for revival without even defining what revival really is. (If you ask one hundred prayerful saints what revival is, you will probably get one hundred different answers.) Some define revival as spiritual manifestations (as in Toronto and Pensacola). Others classify revival as souls getting saved—something I classify as an awakening (when sinners are saved).

Regardless of all the definitions of revival that are out there, the simplest definition of revival I think most of us can agree on is *revive*—*re* meaning "again," and *vive* meaning "to live" (to resuscitate it). In my understanding of the Scriptures, revival is for God's people (shown in Psalm 85:4–6 and in the revivals of King Josiah,

1

Hezekiah and Jehoshaphat) to re-awaken them to go forth in a commitment to serve God. But is that really an end goal? If someone has to be revived, then they obviously are backslidden. In other words, revival shouldn't be an end; it should be the norm for the church—the starting point for us as Christians to begin to really do the work of the gospel. With that being the case, what then should we be praying for?

CHAPTER 2

THE MISSION OF THE CHURCH

In Matthew 6:10, Jesus gave the body of Christ our mission for our stay in the earth. He taught us that when we pray, the essence, the motive and the purpose of our prayer to the Father should be, "Thy kingdom come. Thy will be done in earth, as it is in heaven."

Jesus was very purposeful. The first time He ministered (and I believe the first time He ministered in any new location), He read from the prophet Isaiah and gave His vision statement to all the people (Luke 4:18–19). He was extremely goal centered. In Luke 13:32 He called Herod a fox, and then in verse 33 He told anybody that was listening that He would not be stopped from reaching His goal of going to Jerusalem. Finally, in John 18:37 He plainly laid out to Pilate the purpose of why He came to the earth:

> Pilate therefore said unto him, Art thou a king then? Jesus answered, Thou sayest that I am a king. To this end was I born, and for this cause came I into the world, that I should bear witness unto the truth. Every one that is of the truth heareth my voice.

This purpose-driven and goal-centered visionary certainly wouldn't leave His followers without a sense of mission and purpose, would He? I believe not!

The one clear mission statement for everyone in the body of Christ, regardless of their gifts and calling, is clearly stated here—to do His will on earth as it is in heaven. Jesus was saying that the frame of reference we all should have, regardless of our denominational affiliation, is to reflect heaven on earth. Why? Because in heaven the rebellion has been cast out (Rev. 12:9). It is the only place in the whole universe that is presently a model of what an abode would look like that was finally under the reign of God.

The mission for Christians is to put down rebellion on earth and reflect on earth that which Scripture says is in heaven.

CHAPTER 3

THE PURPOSE OF THE CROSS

If you were to ask one hundred different Christians in this day and age why the Lord Jesus died on the cross, probably 99.9 percent of them would say that it was so they can go to heaven.

This comes out of a self-centered, individualistic culture that has brainwashed the church. The main purpose of Jesus dying on the cross was not so that you can go to heaven. The main purpose of His death was so that His kingdom can be established in you so that, as a result, you can exercise kingdom authority on the earth (Luke 17:21) and reconcile the world back unto Him (2 Corinthians 5:19).

God commanded us clearly in Matthew 6:33 to seek first His kingdom (the King's dominion) and His righteousness (the result of submitting to His rule). Am I saying that His atonement didn't make a way for me to go to heaven? Of course not! I am simply saying that our going to heaven wasn't the main focal point of the cross but simply a by-product of the main purpose—the establishing of God's kingdom on earth. If the kingdom of heaven comes in you, you'll go to heaven anyway! If our only goal is to go to heaven, it's self-centered and ignores the greater purpose of the lordship of Christ over all the earth.

CHAPTER 4

THE GOSPEL OF THE KINGDOM OR THE GOSPEL OF AMERICAN CULTURE

As God is uniting thousands of pastors together, many pastors are getting excited as if that's the only thing we need to do before Jesus comes back. The way I look at it, it's exciting because it's a step in the right direction. It should be normal for pastors and churches to be working together. But it is still just the beginning of the journey. We are just getting warmed up. We haven't even played the game yet.

Because of our American culture and history (the War for Independence), some of our greatest strengths (the pursuit of liberty and justice) have been perverted and have become a great weakness. Since the birth of our nation we have increasingly glorified rugged individualism and rebellion. Our greatest cinema heroes are Rambo, John Wayne, Clint Eastwood, Action Jackson, Steven Seagal—men who go into an arena of conflict totally outnumbered and out-gunned but still come out on top. In real life Rambo gets killed as soon as he falls out of the helicopter, and John Wayne gets beat up or shot dead in that bar fight! It would be cute if these were just limited to imaginary screen roles, but unfortunately, that independent superstar mentality has crept into the church.

The result of all of this is in the church today. We still have key people disconnected from the local vision, pastors disconnected from one another and a host of churches disconnected from the historic church, leaving them without a biblical understanding of purpose and without a right picture of what the kingdom of God is all about.

Most of our preaching and teaching is individualistic, myopic (only see yourself) and vertical. But Matthew 22:37–39 teaches us that it also needs to be horizontal (across or lateral) and corporate. We have superstar preachers and mega-churches that seem to be islands unto themselves, trying to take on the enemy alone. People are just laboring to build their own empire. To further exacerbate the "I, me and my" mentality in the church, many bestsellers in

Christian bookstores stress self-help, self-image and self-esteem (instead of dying to self and developing a Christ consciousness in our lives and a biblical world-view for society).

Many preachers only emphasize how to believe God for *my* miracle! As a young minister, because of the abovementioned paradigm, my goal was eventually to have such a powerful ministry that I would fill stadiums and usher in revival in city after city until Jesus came back. It wasn't until I went through a period of severe testing and suffering in the late 1980s that I realized I needed other pastors in my community to survive and that only together would we be able to take our cities for God. I even started to interpret the Bible differently—realizing that when Paul wrote to the Romans, Corinthians, Ephesians, Colossians and Philippians, he was writing to "the *church* of Ephesus," not to the *churches* of Ephesus or to individuals in the local churches. I realized that I couldn't interpret the Bible correctly unless I had a corporate biblical presupposition as a starting point.

The chart on the following page shows three scriptures with two different ways to interpret the verses. In order to get the true meaning of Isaiah 61:1, you need to read Isaiah 61:4.

> And they shall build the old wastes, they shall raise up the former desolations, and they shall repair the waste cities, the desolations of many generations.

Before anyone gets concerned, I am not saying that we cannot extract principles from Scripture and apply them to us personally, but I am saying that the proper way to do so is through the lens of the corporate church. In other words, I just can't do my own thing, give just where I want and be disconnected from the local church. I will only truly be blessed and reach my potential when I understand that my individual destiny is wrapped up in the destiny of the local church, and the local church will be blessed as the city church gets blessed!

So you can see extreme individualism has even negatively affected the way we interpret Scripture. I'll go a step further. Local churches can't even claim the fullness of Philippians 1:6 and 4:19 without being involved with the greater body of Christ in their community!

There is a Philippians 1:6 promise for the local church—but

He which hath begun a good work in you will perform it until the day of Jesus Christ.

—PHILIPPIANS 1:6

BIBLICAL:

Paul was speaking to the whole church.

This verse will only be fulfilled if I stay in fellowship in the local church.

AMERICAN CULTURE:

Paul was just speaking to me.

This verse will be fulfilled if I quote it and believe it regardless if I am faithful or not in a local church.

But my God shall supply all your need according to his riches in glory by Christ Jesus.

—PHILIPPIANS 4:19

BIBLICAL:

This was a promise to the whole church because as a church they gave a financial gift to Paul.

God only prospers somebody if they add to God's kingdom by blessing the local church.

God wants to prosper a whole church with the result being that all the people would prosper as well.

AMERICAN CULTURE:

This is something just for me if I give tithes and offerings.

If I confess this and believe it and give where I feel led God will provide all my needs.

God wants to prosper my family and me.

The Spirit of the Lord GOD is upon me; because the LORD hath anointed me to preach good tidings unto the meek; he hath sent me to bind up the brokenhearted, to proclaim liberty to the captives, and the opening of the prison to them that are bound.

—ISAIAH 61:1

BIBLICAL:

The purpose of the anointing is to release individuals from bondage so they will transform whole cities.

AMERICAN CULTURE:

The purpose of the anointing is to demonstrate God's miracle power so that we can have a powerful ministry and get many individuals to heaven.

there is an even greater Philippians 1:6 promise when you see and work interdependently with the city church. Our motto should be "One City, One Church!"

Being Born Again

One more verse I want to bring out. (Hopefully the following won't be so radical to you that it will turn you off and then you tune me out.) Most of us have presented at one time or another that familiar portion of Scripture in John 3:3: "Except a man be born again, he cannot see the kingdom of God." Because of our individualistic paradigm, we have all interpreted that verse through the lens of our self-centered culture; we have preached what we thought Jesus meant—"You must be born again to go to heaven."

Although it is certainly true that we must be born again to go to heaven, a second look shows us that we are misquoting the verse. It says that we must be born again to *see the kingdom of God*. The main purpose of evangelism is to open up the spiritual eyes of all people, get them to submit to the lordship of Christ and to see the King's dominion over His entire kingdom, and then draft people into His kingdom army!

For example, before our regeneration we thought it was man's world—that we evolved by chance into what we are right now; that our father was a one-cell amoeba; that our uncle is a tree and that the universe came into existence as a result of some big bang! The greatest thing that happens when you receive Jesus into your life for salvation is that you begin to see the whole earth as belonging to the Lord and Jesus Christ as the rightful ruler over all creation.

> The earth is the LORD's, and the fulness thereof; the world, and they that dwell therein.
>
> —PSALM 24:1

This brings us to the next question—what is the kingdom of God?

CHAPTER 5

THE KINGDOM OF GOD

If you were to ask one hundred different Christians what the kingdom of God is, you would probably get about fifty different answers.

The most common belief of the saints is that the kingdom of God is the church. While this is partially true, it is not the whole truth. The truth of the matter is that the church is in the kingdom, but the kingdom is much larger than the church. The church is the primary agent, its representative with the authority of the kingdom, but the kingdom of God is much more than the church. It encompasses all of the reign of God both in heaven and on earth. This is perhaps the most misunderstood truth in the Bible and something the enemy has done to cause the church to be confused as to its mission.

For the sake of clarity let me define the term *kingdom.* It comes from two words—*king* and *domain.* The Bible teaches us in Revelation 19:16 that Jesus is King of kings. Revelation 1:5 calls Jesus "the prince of the kings of the earth," meaning the rulers on the earth right now. Jesus declared Himself a king in John 18:37. Paul calls Him the "only Potentate, the King of kings, and Lord of lords" (1 Tim. 6:15). Ephesians 1:21 says that Jesus is "far above all principality, and power, and might, and dominion, and every name that is named, not only in this world, but also in that which is to come." And Philippians 2:10–11 commands every knee to bow and every tongue to confess that Jesus Christ is Lord in heaven and on earth. Psalm 24:1 tells us that "the earth is the LORD's." Psalm 96:10 declares that God reigns among the nations. Numerous psalms have declared the rule of God over earth over and over again.

So with Scripture so clear on the subject, why the confusion? Why is it that so many Christians live and act as though the rule of the Lord is just for the church or for the next life? Could it be because there is a misinterpretation of the Scriptures?

Let's look at some examples:

> And you hath he quickened, who were dead in trespasses
> and sins; wherein in time past ye walked according to the

11

course of this world, according to the prince of the power
of the air, the spirit that now worketh in the children of disobedience: Among whom also we all had our conversation
in times past in the lusts of our flesh, fulfilling the desires
of the flesh and of the mind; and were by nature the children of wrath, even as others.

—EPHESIANS 2:1–3

And we know that we are of God, and the whole world
lieth in wickedness.

—1 JOHN 5:19

These verses basically teach that the world system is presently
being influenced and controlled by the enemy, but nowhere in
Scripture does it say that Satan has the right to continue to do this!
I contend that Jesus told us in the Lord's Prayer to make earth
reflect heaven—to seek first His kingdom and His righteousness. I
believe this means our mission is not simply to disciple people to
make it to heaven, but also to put down the present satanic system
and declare, "The kingdom of God is at hand" (inaugurated now).
(See Matthew 4:17; 12:28.)

This means more than just casting devils out of people; it means
also casting devils out of the system, families, neighborhoods, communities, cities and even nations. According to Colossians 2:15
Jesus already has disarmed Satan. Now it's up to the church to "displace him"!

Here's another misunderstood scripture:

Again, the devil taketh him up into an exceeding high
mountain, and sheweth him all the kingdoms of the world,
and the glory of them; and saith unto him, All these things
will I give thee, if thou wilt fall down and worship me.
Then saith Jesus unto him, Get thee hence, Satan; for it is
written, Thou shalt worship the Lord thy God, and him
only shalt thou serve.

—MATTHEW 4:8–10

It is said that because Jesus didn't dispute what Satan said, He
was saying in essence that the devil owns the world. Let me repeat
my earlier statement: Satan has influence over political and societal systems, but Jesus never said he had the right! In fact, Jesus said
the opposite! He told Satan in the context of the kingdoms of the
world that Scripture teaches we should worship (not meaning

singing songs but submitting to) the Lord our God. He wasn't just talking about Himself or the devil, but He was referring to the kingdoms of this world! In other words, Jesus was plainly saying here that the kingdoms of the world should worship (submit to) God!

CHAPTER 6

THE REAL REASON THEY CRUCIFIED JESUS

A fundamental thing for us to understand before we go any further is why Jesus was crucified. In other words, what was the motive behind the Jewish and the Roman power base in their actions against our Lord? I used to think Jesus was crucified and the early church was persecuted because they believed in a new religion. The truth of the matter is that Roman culture was imbued with polytheism (the worship of many gods). They didn't care about another religion. They crucified Jesus and persecuted the early church because the church understood that the earth is the Lord's and that Jesus is the King over all the rulers of the earth. (For more information, read *How Should We Then Live?* by Francis Schaeffer.[1]) The Sanhedrin wanted Jesus dead because He threatened their power base. Herod tried to kill Jesus when He was an infant because Jesus was born the king of the Jews. (See Matthew 2:1–3, 16.) When Pilate sought to release Jesus, the Jews knew what to say to provoke Pilate and get Jesus killed: "Whoever maketh himself a king speaketh against Caesar" (John 19:12).

Later on in the Book of Acts, the disciples disrupted the economic, political and social base of every city they went to because the culture was inextricably interwoven with idol worship and emperor worship. Wherever they went, they turned the world (*kosmos*, world system) upside down.

> And when they found them not, they drew Jason and certain brethren unto the rulers of the city, crying, These that have *turned the world upside down* are come hither also; whom Jason hath received: and these all do *contrary to the decrees of Caesar*, saying that *there is another king*, one Jesus. And they *troubled the people* [economically and socially] and the *rulers of the city* [politically], when they heard these things.
>
> —ACTS 17:6–8, EMPHASIS ADDED

It saddens me that we are missing the mission of our church because of myopic preaching and poor hermeneutics (the science of interpreting Scripture).

The present church acts as though Jesus is only Lord over the church. My Bible clearly teaches He is the ruler of all the princes of the earth. He is King of kings and Lord of lords—the only potentate. (See 1 Timothy 6:15.)

That means that not only the church—not only the saved—but also even the unredeemed are accountable to Jesus as Lord whether they like it or not! God commands all men everywhere to submit to King Jesus and repent (Acts 17:30).

God is requiring that all earthly laws and politicians submit to His rule and reflect biblical principles of law for society and government. There is only one lawgiver and judge (James 4:12), and they must reflect this in their policies or they will be judged!

It saddens me when I hear a so-called Christian politician say that even though he is pro-life privately, he is pro-choice publicly because he can't force his views on others. What these leaders must understand is that God does not dichotomize between personal and public policy. Your personal faith must also include principles that are to be adhered to in public policy or it isn't worth anything! (Of course, in an open society such as the United States we are talking about reflecting biblical principles—not using legislation in a way that forces people to convert.)

Ultimately, our mayors, governors, congress, president, supreme government and all public and private citizens are all required by God to submit in this life to the reign and rule of God.

> Be wise now therefore, O ye kings; be instructed, ye judges of the earth. Serve the LORD with fear, and rejoice with trembling. Kiss the Son, lest he be angry, and ye perish from the way, when his wrath is kindled but a little. Blessed are all they that put their trust in him.
>
> —PSALM 2:10–12

CHAPTER 7

THE NATURE OF THE CHURCH
AND THE GRAND COMMISSION

As stated in previous chapters, there has been much misinterpretation of Scripture—especially when it has to do with the reign of God. In this chapter I will set forth another major misunderstanding—the role and nature of the church.

To start off, let's look at the word Lord Jesus used to describe the assembly of His people in the New Testament. The first usage of the word *church* in the Bible is found in Matthew 16:18: "Upon this rock I will build my church; and the gates of hell shall not prevail against it."

The Greek word for *church* is *ekklesia*. This term *ekklesia* was not original; it was already in use in Greek culture to describe the assembly of Greek citizens in free states who came together to make policy decisions for the city. These people, the *ekklesia*, came together to vote in elected officials, to declare war and to form policy for the operation of the city. In summary, these were the people who ran the city. They didn't come together just to sing songs, get hyped up, shout and have other worldly experiences; they came together to rule! An example of this in scripture is found in Acts 19:23–41 when the community in Ephesus came together to discuss what to do about Paul. Note especially verses 32, 39 and 41 where the word *assembly* is the Greek word *ekklesia*.

In keeping with the purpose of His coming as a king (John 18:37) to rule, He obviously needed to raise up people with delegated authority to carry out His rule on the earth. If you don't understand this, you won't understand the most basic concept of the church. God isn't primarily excited over great sermons, great worship services and people falling down under the power. God is more interested in what we do when we get off the floor! If we get up still living by a pagan humanistic world-view, then we are missing the main reason for the gospel of the kingdom, the cross and the very existence of the church!

If our only calling in life is just to worship God and be intimate

with Him, then He would have told us in Matthew 6:33 to seek first
His face. But rather He said to seek first His kingdom. If all that
mattered to God was our personal piety, then the Lord's prayer just
would have instructed us to say, "Hallowed by thy name." It would
have left out, "Thy will be done, on earth as it is in heaven." If
that's the case, we may as well get raptured as soon as we get saved,
because the worship is much better in heaven than it is on earth!
You get the picture by now, don't you? (Besides, if you really are
seeking first His kingdom, it starts by seeking first His face and His
rule over you personally!)

When Christians make statements like "I don't know if
Christians should get involved in politics," I laugh. Don't they know
the very word *church* (*ekklesia*) has strong political connotations?

When you are in the *ekklesia*, you are a politician involved in the
activities of both the spiritual and natural beings that influence the
political and social structure of our world. When people wonder if
the church should be involved in social issues, it shows that they
are ignorant of the wholistic nature and calling of the church. The
same people who question whether or not the church should be
involved in job training, housing, mentoring, empowering the poor
and community development are people who must obviously live
in affluent neighborhoods. If you lived in a rat-infested, disease-
breeding apartment building, you would never ask if the gospel
should affect our social surroundings. Those who question this and
live in nice neighborhoods are the same people who teach their
children that they have a nice car, nice house and a good job
because God has blessed them—so you see, they really do believe
in a social gospel!

Let me make this one thing clear: I do believe in the separation
of church and state. I don't believe any one church or denomina-
tion should run civic government, but I do not believe in the separation of God and state. God requires all leaders to rule under the
standard of His law and rule.

> By me kings reign, and princes decree justice…I lead in the
> way of righteousness, in the midst of the paths of judgment.
> —Proverbs 8:15, 20

> But we know that the law is good, if a man use it lawfully;
> knowing this, that the law is not made for a righteous man,
> but for the lawless and disobedient, for the ungodly and for

sinners, for unholy and profane, for murderers of fathers
and murderers of mothers, for manslayers, for whoremon-
gers, for them that defile themselves with mankind, for
menstealers, for liars, for perjured persons, and if there be
any other thing that is contrary to sound doctrine.

—1 TIMOTHY 1:8–10

Matthew 16:18 tells us, "The gates of hell shall not prevail against
[the *ekklesia*]." Jesus makes it very clear here that His *ekklesia* will
be in conflict with the gates (the word used to describe the main
power base of cities, including the economical, educational, political and judicial). This is the place the leaders of the city met to make
decisions, set policy, place leadership and declare war (for example,
city hall)—all the things the *ekklesia* is supposed to do.

By saying that the gates shall not prevail, Jesus was using a political and social buzzword, a term used to describe the epicenter for
every realm "of life" in a city. Jesus makes it absolutely clear here
that His will for His *ekklesia* is to displace the power base of the
enemy with His rule.

And they blessed Rebekah, and said unto her, Thou art our
sister, be thou the mother of thousands of millions, and let
thy seed possess the gate of those which hate them.

—GENESIS 24:16

Then shall the father of the damsel, and her mother, take
and bring forth the tokens of the damsel's virginity unto the
elders of the city in the gate…Judges and officers shalt
thou make thee in all thy gates, which the Lord thy God
giveth thee, throughout thy tribes; and they shall judge the
people with just judgment.

—DEUTERONOMY 22:15; 16:18

Scripture clearly teaches us that we are called to possess the
gates of our enemies.

That in blessing I will bless thee, and in multiplying I will
multiply thy seed as the stars of the heaven, and as the sand
which is upon the sea shore; and thy seed shall possess the
gate of his enemies.

—GENESIS 22:17

Lift up your heads, O ye gates; and be ye lift up, ye everlasting doors; and the King of glory shall come in. Who is

the King of glory? The LORD strong and mighty, the LORD
mighty in battle. Lift up your heads, O ye gates; even lift
them up, ye everlasting doors; and the King of glory shall
come in. Who is this King of glory? The LORD of hosts, he
is the King of glory.

—PSALM 24:7–10

Most pastors are happy if they just have good attendance and
have a good meeting. That is not God's goal for us. God is interested in one thing—that the principalities, powers and rulers of the
darkness of this age be broken in the gates so that the gospel will
penetrate every facet of society!

Possessing the gates means that the Word of God should be the
standard (administered by godly leadership) for everything the
gates represented and controlled. In other words, God has called
for His Word to be the standard not only in our churches but also
in economics, science, education and politics—everything dealt
with in the gates!

CHAPTER 8

ARE YOU LOOKING FOR ANTICHRIST OR FOR THE VICTORIOUS CHRIST?

I've heard it said many times, "I know we win because I've read the end of the book." That is partially true. I know we win because I've read the beginning of the book (Gen. 1:26–28), the middle of the book (Matt. 16:18) and the end of the book (Rev. 21–22).

In Genesis 1:26–28 God told Adam to have dominion, to bear fruit and multiply, and to subdue the earth. God was essentially saying to Adam, "You and your seed will manage Planet Earth for me. You will rule it and subdue the earth so that the whole earth is under the rule of God the way it is in that geographic area known as the Garden of Eden." (See Psalm 115:16.) The mere fact that God gave Adam that mandate shows that there must have been demonic hosts in other parts of the earth that he was called to subdue and overcome! (The Edenic theme is in other parts of Scripture such as Ezekiel 36:35—"And they shall say, This land that was desolate is become like the garden of Eden; and the waste and desolate and ruined cities are become fenced, and are inhabited.")

Even though Adam sinned, that covenant of dominion God made with Adam was never taken away in any subsequent covenants:

- Not in the covenant with Noah (Gen. 9:1–2, 7, where the Adamic covenant was reconfirmed)

- Not in the covenant with Abraham (Gen. 12:2–3; 17:2; 22:17)

- Not in the Law of Moses (Deut. 28:13)

- Not in the Davidic covenant (2 Sam. 7:16)

- Not in the covenant with Solomon (1 Kings 8:56–60; 9:5)

- And certainly not in the New Covenant (which was founded upon even better promises and had the Great Commission, a command to bring whole nations under the rule of God as God originally intended in Genesis 1:26–28)

> And Jesus came and spake unto them, saying, All power is given unto me in heaven and in earth. Go ye therefore, and teach all nations, baptizing them in the name of the Father, and of the Son, and of the Holy Ghost: Teaching them to observe all things whatsoever I have commanded you: and, lo, I am with you alway, even unto the end of the world.
> —MATTHEW 28:18–20

Teaching (Greek, "to disciple") the nations is not talking about merely bringing individuals to Christ. The Greek meaning of "nations" is a collection of people who share the same kinds of food, money, language and culture. It's talking about tribes of people; henceforth it has a corporate meaning and refers to whole nations—not individuals. I dare anybody to show me a scripture that does away with this mandate and this purpose! (The prayer movement is just the precursor to clear the air so that the ground troops can move in and take over.)

You might ask, "What about the Antichrist?" There is much scriptural and historical debate over whether the Book of Revelation is historical or yet to be fulfilled. However, even if you believe Revelation is primarily futuristic, you must understand that Antichrist only rules ten nations in the old Roman Empire. He only has complete rule for three and one-half years, and those obscure scriptures in Revelation cannot possibly do away with the overwhelming amount of scripture that clearly gives a victorious motif for the church!

Without getting into it fully at this time, let me just say that hyper-dispensational eschatology that just focuses the church on the Rapture and looking toward gloom and doom and Antichrist have caused much harm to the body of Christ! This extreme teaching has historically (since the 1880s) slowly gotten the churches away from trying to promote the kingdom of God in our cities. If you believe the church is doomed to failure and the Antichrist is going to take over everything, then why try to reform our cities? Why get involved in politics? Why build inter-generationally for our children? Why minister in the poorest neighborhoods if you're just supposed to look for the Rapture?

The general themes of Scripture clearly refute this. Whether you

are amillennial, premillennial or postmillennial, you can still desire
to disciple the nations, restore the old waste places (Isa. 58:12) and
have a victorious view of the future for the church. You can be premillennial, amillennial or postmillennial, but please don't be
"pessimillennial" (a term I heard Dr. John Kelly use describing the
pessimistic, defeatist view of many present-day saints). Isaiah
9:6–7 sums up the victorious mandate of the church beautifully.

> For unto us a child is born, unto us a son is given: and the
> government shall be upon his shoulder: and his name shall
> be called Wonderful, Counsellor, The mighty God, The
> everlasting Father, The Prince of Peace. Of the increase of
> his government and peace there shall be no end, upon the
> throne of David, and upon his kingdom, to order it, and to
> establish it with judgment and with justice from henceforth
> even forever. The zeal of the LORD of hosts will perform this.

Notice that "of the increase of His government there shall be no
end," so no matter what the future holds, God's government and
His rule will always increase as time goes on, not decrease!

What Are You Believing For?

For too long the church has individualized the gospel and just
believed God for individual forgiveness of sin, physical healing, a
nice car or a nice house. I have no problem with believing God for
those things. My only problem with that is that it doesn't go far
enough! God has called us to use our faith for greater things than
these! At stake are our communities, cities and whole nations! If the
devil can get us just to use our faith for individual needs, whole
cities will be destroyed and neglected because of our lack of biblical
purpose.

The Bible teaches us in Matthew 6:33 that if we seek first His
kingdom and His righteousness, all of our individual needs will be
met anyway!

What the Scriptures Teach About Taking Cities and Nations for God

> Ask of me, and I shall give thee the heathen for thine inheri-
> tance, and the uttermost parts of the earth for thy possession.

Thou shalt break them with a rod of iron; thou shalt dash
them in pieces like a potter's vessel.

—Psalm 2:8–9

This psalm is a key verse all Christians need to understand if we
are going to understand the past two thousand years of world history and if we are going to understand the purpose of the New
Testament church. This is a messianic psalm that promises the
nations to Christ. This psalm clearly teaches us to believe God to
exercise our faith in prayer for the purpose of subduing whole
nations for God. You might say this is a messianic psalm promising
the nations to Christ, not to the church.

However, Romans 8:17 clearly teaches us that we are coheirs
(joint-heirs) with Christ. In other words, whatever the Father
promised the Son He also conferred upon His church. We are so
implicitly identified with Christ that whatever happened to Christ
happened to us as well! When Jesus was crucified we were crucified. When Jesus was raised we were raised. When Jesus was glorified we were glorified. (See Romans 6; 8:29; Ephesians 1:17; 2:6.)
Whatever the Father has caused the Son to inherit, we as the
church also inherit! Lord Jesus is the head of the body—the
church. We are so intricately interwoven in the Son as His body
that the church is called "the fullness of him who fills everything
in every way" (Eph. 1:23, NIV). In other words, God has ordained
the church to be the entity He uses to fill the earth, inherit the
nations and subdue the earth (disciple the nations) with His glory.

Hebrews 11 is called the Faith's Hall of Fame because it gives us
snapshots of the greatest biblical heroes of faith the world has ever
known. Those people mentioned by name were not mentioned for
their ability to believe God for themselves, for their needs to be met
or for personal miracles. These people were mentioned because
their faith was used to shake and shape nations!

Men like Noah, Abraham, Jacob, Joseph, Moses, Gideon, Barak,
Samson, Jepthah, David and Samuel all had faith that shook whole
kingdoms. You might say that was only for the Old Testament. If it
was not meant for the church to emulate, then why was it written to
us? Why does the Book of Hebrews admonish us to follow those who
through patience and faith inherit the promises (Heb. 6:12)? Why is
it that throughout the Church Age we have seen God raise up people
who literally shaped nations with their faith and obedience? In this

last millennium men like John Hus, John Wycliffe, Martin Luther, John Calvin, Count Nikolaus Zinzendorf, John Wesley, George Whitfield, William Wilberforce, Charles Simeon, Charles Finney, D. L. Moody and Abraham Kuyper, and in our day men like Martin Luther King Jr. and James Dobson, have made a major political, social and ecclesiastical impact!

To sum it up, Hebrews 11:33 tells us they used their faith to subdue kingdoms! This wasn't after this life was over, but during this life! If their faith was just used to help themselves as individuals, then their influence would have never been felt in the nations!

Revelation 2:26–27 promises overcomers who keep His works until the end (Greek *telos*, to its furthest end; maturity; completion, not necessarily talking about physical death) that they will have power over the nations and that they would exercise rule over them. Sounds like the passages on possessing the gates, doesn't it?

Psalm 85:9 tells us that we are saved so that God's glory will dwell in our land (not just our homes!)

Second Chronicles 7:14 teaches us that if God's people (those with the Genesis 1:28 commission) would corporately humble themselves, pray, seek God's face and turn from evil, the result would be that God heals our *land*, not just our physical bodies!

We are not called to be a nice Christian social club; we are commanded to take the kingdom by force, or proactively engaging the gates of the enemy in spiritual and cultural warfare (Matt. 11:12).

Instead of actively engaging the enemy by prayer and by developing leadership equipped to rule in the gates, we have a majority of evangelical Christians buying the latest books on prophecy (many based on the changing winds of newspaper headlines without incorporating proper biblical hermeneutics) and talking about when the Rapture will take place. The enemy would like nothing better than for the church to focus on a way to escape this world rather than engage the gates of hell in hand-to-hand spiritual and cultural warfare!

Without getting into a lot of eschatological specifics, let me just repeat what I say to our congregation all the time: I don't believe Jesus is coming back in the next few years because I don't think He's coming back until we complete our mission! He's not coming back to a church subsumed by the world, selfishly looking for Jesus to do all the work He commissioned the church to do! He's not coming back until we complete our mission! He's coming back for "a glorious church, not having spot, or wrinkle" (Eph. 5:27), a victorious church that will bring honor to His name. My Bible tells me clearly that Jesus isn't coming back until His enemies are under His feet (Ps. 110:1).

This does not mean everybody in the world will be saved, but that the church possesses the gates of hell and exerts kingdom influence in the nations! God made a covenant with His people to use them to bless the families of the earth (Acts 3:25) and that the heavens will retain Jesus until the restoration of all things.

> Whom the heaven must receive until the times of restitution of all things, which God hath spoken by the mouth of all his holy prophets since the world began.
>
> —Acts 3:21

Sounds like the Genesis 1:26–28 and Matthew 28:19–20 mandate!

CHAPTER 9

DO YOU HAVE A PLATONIC RELATIONSHIP WITH GOD AND THE WORLD?

I believe with all my heart in personal piety. I spend more time in prayer than I do anything else in my life. Though I believe that intimacy with God is by far the most important thing to strive for as a Christian, I also know that the second of the greatest commandments is also in the Bible—love your neighbor as you love yourself. The Bible tells us in the fourth and fifth chapters of 1 John that the proof that we love the God that we can't see is that we love those we can see. (There will always be a physical manifestation of your spiritual essence.) Although we can trace the following imbalances all the way to the monastic reformation movement in the sixth century, for now we will just deal with the modern roots of pietism going back to the early eighteenth century with Philipp Jakob Spener and August Francke (with the power base centered in the University of Halle).

Pietism was a reaction to the formalized, dead, ritualistic church that allowed you to be a church member if you lived in a certain geographic area. The Lutherans believed in the state church; in order to be a citizen of good standing, you had to be a member of the Lutheran Church, even if you were unconverted in your heart.

Though Pietism was an important move of God, people took it to the extreme and became focused only on their inward relationship with God to the neglect of societal reform and outward works. Politics and social reform were looked upon as unimportant because they weren't "as spiritual." The result was that many in church embraced a "new Gnosticism"—the platonic classical Greek philosophy that basically taught that the material world was evil and that only the spiritual world was good. Gnosticism taught that true religion is about trying to rid yourself of all material influences so that you can be spiritual and please God.

The expression "having a platonic relationship with someone" means that your relationship is based solely on the higher ideals of the joining of your spirits and emotions; it does not include an intimate physical interaction. Many saints have truly become so "heavenly minded that they really are no earthly good." They presently have a "platonic relationship" with God and the world. The problem with platonic relationships is that it doesn't reproduce after its own kind; it remains "barren." Much of the church has been captivated by the influence of this Gnostic classical Greek influence, and they don't even realize it!

In their ignorance they have a platonic relationship with God and man, and they don't understand the great biblical imbalances with that world-view! It seems that many evangelicals read Matthew 24 (chapter on End-Time prophecy), skip Matthew 25 (containing the passage about believers expressing and proving their faith by ministering to the physical needs of people) and then read Matthew 26 on!

We have to realize that there are over five hundred scriptures in the Bible on ministering to the poor, and only two passages on the virgin birth! Many, many scriptures admonish us to be involved with societal justice. Isaiah 61:1–4 teaches us that the proof we are anointed is not speaking in tongues or preaching—but building up the old waste places of the cities, thus returning them back to the standard God shows us in His Word.

CHAPTER 10

THE NEXT MOVE: INCARNATION

We talked about the imbalances of pietism in the last chapter. Now let's talk about what I believe is about to happen in the next move of God.

The last ten years have seen an incredible move of God in the church. Thousands of leaders and churches are getting together as never before for Concerts of Prayer, spiritual warfare, spiritual mapping and prayer walking. If you listen closely, the theme for all of this prayer worldwide is for a revival that will spread across the world and imbue the earth with God's glory and rule. Many leaders in the church think that the Holy Spirit is mainly setting us up to meet the Antichrist or the New World Order—I disagree! I believe God is setting us up for victory all over the earth!

If you really examine the prayer movement (especially spiritual mapping) and take it to its furthest end, you can only come to one conclusion. The purpose of spiritual mapping is so that we can have dominion in every facet of society. Furthermore, examine the words of much of the popular Christian music put out the last ten years, and you will see the same theme over and over again—the declaration of the kingdom of God and the defeat of the enemy in our lands! I ask, Why not? True spiritual dominance will always result in a physical manifestation of that dominance! Church history clearly shows us that as the church goes, so goes a nation's destiny. That all true revivals have always resulted in societal reforms (the revivals of Luther, Calvin, Knox, Finney and others) is a documented fact.

King George III of England even called the American Revolution the Parsons Rebellion. Many have described George Whitefield as the father of the American Revolution because his preaching was the galvanizing force that united the colonies. I once heard a church historian say that the Weslyan revival saved England from a revolution similar to the one France would have in the 1790s.[1] It is also no coincidence that after many fundamental evangelicals fled the cities after the Scopes Monkey Trial in the 1920s the spiritual climate of our cities (left to the liberals who didn't flee) grew much worse! I can go on and on.

I prophesy that the next true move of God in our land (which should naturally follow the prayer movement) will be a social reconstruction and biblical reformation that will transform our cities! Biblical reformation will come to the nations! It will come as a result of the Holy Spirit inspired prayer movement building in nations that will revive the church and cause her to work to establish the principles of God's kingdom "on earth as it is in heaven." The only other alternative will be that nations will learn righteousness as a result of God's judgement (Isa. 26:9)—for example, the former Soviet Union.

The Bible teaches us in John 1:1 that God was the Word—but He didn't stay as the Word. John 1:14 tells us that the Word became flesh and dwelt among us.

Whenever God is about to do something, it always starts off in the spiritual realm and then manifests itself in the physical realm.

> Through faith we understand that the worlds were framed
> by the word of God, so that things which are seen were not
> made of things which do appear.
> —HEBREWS 11:3

What I'm doing in this chapter is taking the kingdom theme of the prayer, praise and prophetic apostolic movement to its furthest end. I believe as Christian leaders we need to start asking ourselves the question (to quote Francis Schaeffer), "How should we then live?" If Jesus is Lord over civic government, economics, education, the arts, media, science and the church…in other words, what would our community, our city, our nation look like (and what would it take to cause this to happen) if Jesus were Lord over our economic, political, educational and religious structure and system? You may say, "That's not for me to think about; if God wants to do it, He'll just do it." With that kind of attitude we are just neglecting the responsibility God gave us in Genesis 1:26–28 of having stewardship over the earth! It also goes against the overall theme of Scripture: God will not do that which He has commanded us to do. If we don't work, neither do we eat! If we don't believe, we perish. Whatever we sow we reap!

> The heaven, even the heavens, are the LORD's: but the earth
> hath he given to the children of men.
> —PSALM 115:16

Instead of just ambiguous praying for revival, we must begin not only to pray specifically with that end in mind but also to begin to position ourselves as a church to be able to take the leadership role after a spiritual awakening hits our cities. This means not only praying but also training and raising up believers in leadership with a biblical world-view in every facet of society, so that after revival hits we will have a wineskin able to hold the wine that God pours out! Otherwise we will experience that which happened in the Welsh revival in the early 1900s. (After an incredible three-year revival it looked as if revival never took place!)

In order to avoid the temporal effectiveness of revival, we need to structure a biblical wineskin that has a broader scope than just the ecclesiastical realm. It must be a wineskin that has answers and leadership for every realm of life so that we not only deal with individual sin but also the whole system. It's a mistake just to emphasize soteriology (personal salvation) and neglect cosmology (universal law).

When God was dealing with Jonah, he was not only concerned with the souls of those under condemnation but also the cattle (cattle represented their economic resources) (Jon. 4:11). The demons begged Jesus to send them into the pigs in Mark 5 because that would have given them a foothold in the economic base of the inhabitants of the Gadarenes. Jesus wants us to overcome the gates of Hades—not just individual demons!

The conclusion of this chapter is this—Are we just looking for a revival, or are we looking for a biblical reformation in the nations that would acknowledge the lordship of Christ and establish God's kingdom in every facet of society? Are we just happy with good meetings, spiritual activity, manifestations and enthusiastic saints, or do we want permanent change for our communities? Do we just want to get millions accepting Jesus as personal Savior without seeing Jesus as their Lord in their everyday life? (This results in Christians who have a world-view that only supports the present pagan structures.)

CHAPTER 11

ARE YOU LIVING IN A GHETTO?

In previous chapters we have already dealt with the issue of the church dichotomizing (separating) the spiritual and the natural in its world-view, thus resulting in a platonic relationship with God and His gospel. In this chapter we are going to examine the consequences of the church embracing only a Utopian spiritual world-view.

As I have already written, the kingdom of God is not the church. The church is in the kingdom; the kingdom of God includes much more than just the church. It signifies the rule of God over all creation!

Let's examine the word *ghetto*. A generation ago, the *ghetto* was a neighborhood in Europe where all Jews were required to live. Now it means a place where only the economically poor are forced to live because they do not have the means to escape.

In this chapter I use the term *ghetto* to signify the church limiting itself to only the spiritual aspects of the planet. The church, because of a narrow understanding of the Bible, has just been preaching the "gospel." However, we are called to preach not just the "gospel" but also the gospel of the kingdom. (The gospel is just good news that Jesus can save you; the gospel of the kingdom not only tells you about salvation, but it also includes the rule of God over all of society and requires all people to submit to the lordship of Christ!)

So the Kingdom of God on earth is this: *The Kingdom of God.*

> The earth is the LORD's and the fulness thereof; the world, and they that dwell therein.
>
> —PSALM 24:1

Although the kingdom of God has implications for the whole earth (including the environment), the present evangelical church primarily concerns itself with things regarding the ecclesiastical realm (the church). The result is that we greatly limit the impact of the gospel and *ghettoize* ourselves into a small component of Planet Earth!

THE PRESENT CHURCH   **THE FUTURE CHURCH**

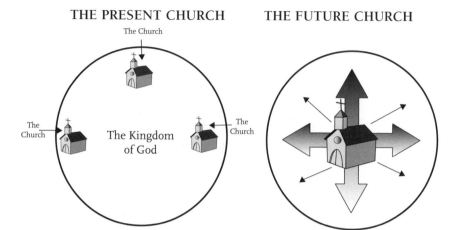

Today's apostles and prophets only emphasize the ecclesiastical realm. We are alone in some unnoticed corner of creation. (We've even been granted a small section in the religious section of our daily newspapers—which clearly illustrates how the world marginalizes believers). The world system is just not threatened when we have our big churches or big evangelistic crusades because our gospel just primarily deals with personal salvation and piety. (They actually like the idea of having nice moral people who advance their pagan, humanistic world-view.)

Christians in this country rarely get persecuted because we don't have a gospel that is wholistic. We treat Jesus as if He's only Lord of the church. The moment we start preaching the gospel of the kingdom and proclaiming the lordship of Christ in civic government, economics, science and education, that's when the conflict will get hot and heavy. That's when we will see the gates of hell challenged!

We need to enlarge the biblical paradigm we presently have of fivefold ministry (apostles, prophets, evangelists, teachers and pastors) to include the concern God has for all of creation. (Haiti doesn't need just another evangelistic crusade; Haiti needs to cast out the spirit of witchcraft and poverty and get apostolic people who use biblical blueprints to rebuild the whole nation.)

In the next move of God, apostles and prophets will be involved in all of creation, not just in the church, because God's kingdom includes all of life. We are going to see apostles and prophets of science, government, economics, technology, businesses, the arts and even the military. Someone might say, "Show me this in the Bible." Moses was called a prophet—yet he didn't only spend time on the mountain with God; he came down from the mountain and administered the political, social, economic, military and Levitical system of Israel.

Joseph, who was called a prophet, basically became the prime minister of Egypt and saved the nation because his prophetic gifting included the word of wisdom for economics and resource management. (We need prophetic people to tell us not only about our sins but also how to invest our money on Wall Street.) The prophet Daniel was second in command to Nebuchadnezzar and probably ran the country while Nebuchadnezzar was dieting on grass for seven years. (See Daniel 4.) Obviously his prophetic ministry had major apostolic implications that involved much more than just praying three times a day in his house (Dan. 6:10).

I believe Nehemiah is a strong Old Testament forerunner of what the New Testament apostle is all about. In rebuilding the wall of Jerusalem he functioned as a master builder that integrated many aspects of life (the social, political, economic and religious spheres of the Jewish people). His ministry was so broad that it also involved a personal grant from King Darius to oversee the bivocational Jewish construction team that would also moonlight as the military.

In rebuilding Jerusalem God used the dynamic triad of Nehemiah (a political, economic leader), Ezra (represented the clergy ecclesiastical) and Esther (a lay person who won the Miss Iran beauty contest). Time doesn't permit me to deal with Abraham, the judges of Israel, Samuel, the kings of Israel and the teaching of the minor prophets. Adam, of course, is the greatest biblical example of the wholistic, all-encompassing nature of the kingdom. Adam walked with God, but as administrator of Planet Earth, he was an expert on animal life (a zoologist who named all the animals) and plant life (botanist), and he was a farmer, a shepherd and probably an astronomer and a teacher. He had to teach his children the ways of the Lord and how to survive and manage the planet.

In the New Testament we don't see the concept as fleshed out, although the theological frame for the gospel of the kingdom is strong. We don't see it fully fleshed out in all of society because the church movement was in its infant stage and needed some time to infiltrate all of society and establish the kingdom of God.

Albeit, the New Testament does show some of this. In Acts 13:1–2 the racially integrated leadership team of Antioch involved two black men (Simeon and Lucius), a real estate dealer (Barnabas, see Acts 4:36–37), a person with political savvy and connections (Manaen) and a former religious leader of Judaism and an intellect (Saul). This paved the way for the gospel to reach every aspect of society in Antioch, which divided its city up according to racial boundaries. The church prior to this was only multilingual; now it was multiethnic! Now the church had the ability to infect all of Antioch and then (using Antioch as a model) the whole world!

Furthermore, Paul, as a master builder, included in his evangelism strategy the goal of winning over the most politically savvy and influential people of urban areas. The following Scripture references will illustrate this:

- A political ruler (Acts 13:6–12)
- A religious leader (Acts 14:13)
- An entrepreneur (Acts 16:14)
- The chief women of the city (Acts 17:4)
- Entrepreneurs (Acts 18:1–3)
- Philosophical leaders (Acts 19:9)
- Honorable women (Acts 17:12)
- Philosophical leaders and teachers (Acts 17:19)
- Chief religious leader (Acts 18:8, 17)
- Chief leaders of Asia (Acts 19:31)
- Two governors (Acts 24:25; 25:12)
- A king (Acts 26:1–8)
- Caesar (Acts 25:10–11)

As we can see in the New Testament, Paul was very successful in reaching the top leadership in every region he ministered in! (See also Philippians 1:13; 4:22, Romans 16:23.) Paul infiltrated the highest levels of government. (Erastus was perhaps the housing developer or mayor of the city.) Furthermore, we see that Paul's ministry disrupted not only the religious systems of his day, but it also affected the political, social and economic systems and leadership.

> But the Jews stirred up the devout and honourable women, and the chief men of the city, and raised persecution against Paul and Barnabas, and expelled them out of their coasts.
> —Acts 13:50

And saying, Sirs, why do ye these things? We also are men of like passions with you, and preach unto you that ye should turn from these vanities unto the living God, which made heaven, and earth, and the sea, and all things that are therein.

—Acts 14:15

And when her masters saw that the hope of their gains was gone, they caught Paul and Silas, and drew them into the marketplace unto the rulers.

—Acts 16:19

And when it was day, the magistrates sent the serjeants, saying, Let those men go. And the keeper of the prison told this saying to Paul, The magistrates have sent to let you go: now therefore depart, and go in peace. But Paul said unto them, They have beaten us openly uncondemned, being Romans, and have cast us into prison; and now do they thrust us out privily? Nay verily; but let them come themselves and fetch us out. And the serjeants told these words unto the magistrates: and they feared, when they heard that they were Romans. And they came and besought them, and brought them out, and desired them to depart out of the city.

—Acts 16:35–39

And when they found them not, they drew Jason and certain brethren unto the rulers of the city, crying, These that have turned the world upside down are come hither also; whom Jason hath received: and these all do contrary to the decrees of Caesar, saying that there is another king, one Jesus. And they troubled the people and the rulers of the city, when they heard these things.

—Acts 17:6–8

And the same time there arose no small stir about that way. For a certain man named Demetrius, a silversmith, which made silver shrines for Diana, brought no small gain unto the craftsmen; whom he called together with the workmen of like occupation, and said, Sirs, ye know that by this craft we have our wealth. Moreover ye see and hear, that not alone at Ephesus, but almost throughout all Asia, this Paul hath persuaded and turned away much people, saying that they be no gods, which are made with hands: So that not only this our craft is in danger to be set at nought; but also

that the temple of the great goddess Diana should be
despised, and her magnificence should be destroyed,
whom all Asia and the world worshippeth. And when they
heard these sayings, they were full of wrath, and cried out,
saying, Great is Diana of the Ephesians. And the whole city
was filled with confusion: and having caught Gaius and
Aristarchus, men of Macedonia, Paul's companions in
travel, they rushed with one accord into the theatre. And
when Paul would have entered in unto the people, the disciples suffered him not. And certain of the chief of Asia,
which were his friends, sent unto him, desiring him that he
would not adventure himself into the theatre. Some therefore cried one thing, and some another, for the assembly
was confused; and the more part knew not wherefore they
were come together. And they drew Alexander out of the
multitude, the Jews putting him forward. And Alexander
beckoned with the hand, and would have made his defence
unto the people. But when they knew that he was a Jew, all
with one voice about the space of two hours cried out,
Great is Diana of the Ephesians. And when the townclerk
had appeased the people, he said, Ye men of Ephesus, what
man is there that knoweth not how that the city of the
Ephesians is a worshipper of the great goddess Diana, and
of the image which fell down from Jupiter? Seeing then
that these things cannot be spoken against, ye ought to be
quiet, and to do nothing rashly. For ye have brought hither
these men, which are neither robbers of churches, nor yet
blasphemers of your goddess. Wherefore if Demetrius, and
the craftsmen which are with him, have a matter against
any man, the law is open, and there are deputies: let them
implead one another. But if ye enquire any thing concern-
ing other matters, it shall be determined in a lawful assembly. For we are in danger to be called in question for this
day's uproar, there being no cause whereby we may give an
account of this concourse. And when he had thus spoken,
he dismissed the assembly.

—ACTS 19:23–41

And when the seven days were almost ended, the Jews
which were of Asia, when they saw him in the temple,
stirred up all the people, and laid hands on him, crying out,
Men of Israel, help: This is the man, that teacheth all men
every where against the people, and the law, and this place:

and further brought Greeks also into the temple, and hath polluted this holy place. (For they had seen before with him in the city Trophimus an Ephesian, whom they supposed that Paul had brought into the temple.) And all the city was moved, and the people ran together: and they took Paul, and drew him out of the temple: and forthwith the doors were shut. And as they went about to kill him, tidings came unto the chief captain of the band, that all Jerusalem was in an uproar. Who immediately took soldiers and centurions, and ran down unto them; and when they saw the chief captain and the soldiers, they left beating of Paul. Then the chief captain came near, and took him, and commanded him to be bound with two chains; and demanded who he was, and what he had done. And some cried one thing, some another, among the multitude; and when he could not know the certainty for the tumult, he commanded him to be carried into the castle.

—ACTS 21:27–34

Some Historical Snapshots

The following are examples of men who functioned as kingdom apostles and prophets, though they may not have actually used the title.

St. Augustine (345–430)

Africa had already given two other great leaders in the church— Cyprian and Tertillian. In response to accusations that the Roman Empire was destroyed because the pagan gods were upset that Rome embraced Christianity, St. Augustine wrote perhaps the most influential book (except for the Bible) in the history of the church—*The City of God*.[1] In this book he gives a theological framework for the "city on a hill"—a city that espouses the kingdom of God in every facet of society. The book was very influential in the lives of many of the great reformers, including John Calvin, Charlemagne and Abraham Kuyper (prime minister of the Netherlands from 1901–1905). His teaching helped shape all of western Christianity.

John Knox (1505–1572)

Within a year of John Knox returning to Scotland (from 1559 to 1560), the Scottish Parliament decreed a change of religion from

Catholicism to Protestantism! The preaching of Knox was powerful. Wherever he preached there followed iconoclastic parties (the
breaking of religious statues). His preaching affected the social,
political, economic and religious atmosphere of his nation!

John Calvin (1509–1564)

From the studying of the Scriptures Calvin realized that God's
glory involved more than saving souls. He believed that the world
was God's world! Therefore he believed in training not only ministers, but also government workers, doctors and lawyers; he
believed all others needed a training that recognized and honored
God. He established the first Protestant University—Geneva
Academy. (It wasn't long before the king of France sent an official
warning to Geneva complaining of all the preachers coming from
this university.) From 1555 on Calvin became the leader of the city
of Geneva, Switzerland. Under his leadership Geneva passed rules
that were designed to guide every aspect of life for its citizens. He
modeled the city after St. Augustine's book *The City of God*.

Abraham Kuyper (1837–1920)

One of the forgotten heroes of the faith amongst today's evangelicals is Abraham Kuyper. While a liberal minister, he was converted by conversations with a pious old lady and was
revolutionized by the writings of Calvin and St. Augustine. As the
book *The City of God* inspired Charlemagne, Pope Gregory VII and
Calvin, so it inspired Kuyper. He labored not only to restore the
church, but also to apply the principles of Christianity to every
domain of life (the political, social, industrial and cultural as well
as the ecclesiastical). He organized a Christian political party and
entered the Dutch Parliament.

In 1880, he founded in Amsterdam a free university based upon
reformation principles. (It was called free because it was free from
the control of church and state.) His influence was so great he actually became the prime minister of the Netherlands from
1901–1905. Kuyper preached, lectured, taught, took part in the
debates of Parliament and wrote. His writing was so profound that
many thousands have learned Dutch in order to read Kuyper's
books in the original language. He inspired thousands not only to
carry the banner of the cross in evangelism, but also to carry the
lordship of Christ into the field of education and politics for social

reformation. He had a healthy balance of emphasizing sound Bible doctrine while at the same time encouraging people to be involved in every aspect of society. He believed in the separation of church and state (the church should not run the government), but not the separation of God's law from state and civic government. Because of Kuyper, Holland experienced a wonderful revival.

John Witherspoon (1722–1794)

He came to America in 1768 to become the president of Princeton College. Has been called the most influential Professor in American History not only because of his powerful oratory but also because of the number of leaders he trained and sent forth. Nine of the fifty-five participants in the Federal convention were his students (including James Madison). Moreover his pupils included a president, vice-president, twenty-one senators, twenty-nine representatives, and fifty-six state legislators, thirty-three judges, three of whom served on the Supreme Court. He was the only clergyman to sign the Declaration of Independence.[2]

Charles Simeon (1759–1836)

Charles Simeon pastored fifty-four years. He wrote books, mentored numerous spiritual leaders, commissioned chaplains and challenged men like Henry Martyn to work for missions. He met weekly for fifty years with William Pitt, William Wilberforce and others to abolish slavery. The British Parliament abolished slavery in England in 1807.[3]

Charles Finney (1792–1875)

This great American revivalist was the catalyst for the Second Great Awakening and an integral part of the Third Great Awakening. His ministry not only touched the working-class people, but he also had a great impact on many influential people, especially among doctors, lawyers and judges. (Examine the Rochester Revival in 1830–1831.) Many of his converts went forth and were involved in societal reform and were the leading advocates of the abolitionist movement (people such as Theodore Weld). Finney became the president of Oberlin College and had as his motivation for ministry the establishing of the kingdom of God on earth.

There are thousands of others we could have used as examples of how God used Christian leadership to shape the whole world. History shows us clearly that as the church goes, so goes the world.

History also shows us how the gospel affects a nation's economics. Most of the poorest countries in the world are those countries that are in the 10/40 window (the nations that have not heard the gospel).

The Buddhist, Hindu and Islamic countries make up 85 percent of the world's poorest countries. Those countries influenced the most by the Protestant Reformation are presently the most prosperous and technologically advanced countries in the earth (for example, the United States, Canada, England, France and Germany). (Refer to Max Weber's *The Protestant Ethic and the Spirit of Capitalism.*[4])

The second most prosperous countries are those that remained primarily Catholic. All this proves the veracity of Psalm 67:5–7 that says that God blesses a land in proportion to the people that praise Him! He prospers His people in every way so that He can establish His covenant in the earth!

> But thou shalt remember the LORD thy God: for it is he that giveth thee power to get wealth, that he may establish his covenant which he sware unto thy fathers, as it is this day.
> —DEUTERONOMY 8:18

History truly is the unfolding of God's purposes. It is a lesson in moral philosophy and kingdom ethics—not just dry facts and events. History is truly His story played out in the earth.

How the Church Became Irrelevant to Society

Up until the 1880s it was common in Protestant Christianity to have a biblical world-view that encompassed every aspect of life. What happened? To summarize it briefly, let me paraphrase from Donald Dayton's book *Discovering an Evangelical Heritage*[5] and give some of my own observations.

Twelve reasons why the evangelical church fled the cities, forsook societal reform and became overly concerned only with individual salvation

1. After people got saved, discipline and a reordered lifestyle enabled converts to prosper and rise in social class, a process resulting in a middle-class church that

became self-centered, forgot their roots and became what the church originally stood against.

2. The destruction of the Civil War caused the body of Christ to abandon their high hopes of establishing the kingdom of God and took away from their reform impulse.

3. After slavery was abolished, the "temperance crusade" (no smoking, no drinking, no gambling) took center stage, translating into more of a concern for personal purity and holiness and an introverted Christianity, which resulted in an internal individualistic emphasis.

4. Massive urbanization (people moving to inner cities) and industrialization brought problems too complex for the revivalist vision of reform.

5. Waves of immigration brought in many people who had no place in this dream of a Protestant Christian America.

6. Increased attacks from outside the church such as the rise of biblical criticism (so called "experts" who questioned the authenticity and reliability of the Bible) and Darwinism (theory of evolution) with its attack on the biblical views of the origin of man caused evangelicalism to turn more and more inward to nurse what remained of their dreams for a Christian America.

7. After the horror of the Civil War, eschatology (biblical teachings of future things) shifted toward a hyper-dispensational view of premillennialism, a belief that doesn't allow for a victorious church that effects lasting societal change but rather sees conditions only worsening for the church and the world. This belief results in a helpless church being raptured right before the Antichrist takes over the world; later the Second Coming of Christ will occur.

    Instead of the hope of the gospel causing societal change, a great emphasis on the power of Satan and sin became prevalent with the only hope for the church being the Rapture! This, of course, resulted in the vision of social reform being replaced with the church looking more for the Second Coming and being rescued from this evil world!

Let me be clear at this point. You can be premillennial, believe that the thousand-year kingdom of God will come after Jesus' bodily return to the earth and still have a victorious view of the future church!

8.   The emergence of extreme dispensational premilleniallism resulted in a wave of excitement about prophecy. The evangelical church then spent much of her energy studying the Bible for the signs of the End Times and in countless "prophecy conferences" (consequently neglecting societal reform). Why should you try to reform society and build for future generations if you think that the Antichrist is going to take it all over anyway?

9.   Pre–Civil War revivalists founded liberal arts colleges. Postwar revivalists founded Bible institutes (not accredited with the state because it only teaches the Bible and leaves out non-biblical studies). This postwar concept of not including the arts in Bible schools further perpetuated the divide between the spiritual and living out our faith in a practical way in the natural world.

10. The rise of fundamentalism and dispensationalism produced an extreme emphasis on the sovereignty of God that took away the biblical balance of human responsibility. For example, in an extreme view of God's sovereignty, if someone is poor, a slave or unconverted, it is because it is God's will; there is nothing the church can or should do about it. By helping the poor, you would be fighting against the lot God ordained for them; by preaching repentance, you're taking away from God's grace and are guilty of preaching works.

11. In the rewriting of church history, modern evangelical editors began to edit out references to social reform. For example, certain messages by Finney, Moody and even the historical teachings of evangelical schools (like Wheaton College) and the movement like the Weslyan Methodists who split from mainline Methodism over the issue of slavery were either totally omitted or blatantly ignored.

12. The Scopes Monkey Trial so humiliated the funda-
    mental evangelical church (they won the judicial trial
    but lost the trial of public opinion) that the 1920s saw
    a mass exodus of fundamentals from the inner cities.
    To this day most Bible schools, mega-churches and
    evangelical Christians live in the suburbs, even though
    today more than half the present population of the
    United States live in the cities (51 percent). In the next
    twenty years 75 percent of our population will be in
    the inner cities! Consequently, societal reform was left
    to the modernists and liberal Christians because they
    stayed in the inner cities.

To this day, many evangelical saints think that if we work for
societal reform we are preaching a "social gospel"—a term consid-
ered anathema in many fundamentalist Bible institutes because a
social gospel is equated mostly with liberal Christianity. (As mentioned before, these same people probably live in a nice suburban
neighborhood. The mere fact that they thank God for their nice
house, nice car and nice neighborhood shows that they believe in
a social gospel!)

I believe the day is coming soon when true apostles, prophets
and ministers of God will be leading the way for societal reform
because they will realize that only the gospel has the blueprint for
a healthy society. Out of the ash heaps of failure because of depending on humanistic philosophies, even the civic leaders will begin to
look for answers from successful apostolic ministries (ministries
that will not only set a drug addict free, but also will turn whole
communities around and be involved in social reconstruction
using the word of God as the guide).

As the problems of the inner city start to spread to the suburbs,
the churches in this millennium that just preach a one-dimensional
individualistic gospel (instead of the gospel of the kingdom) will
have a hard time surviving because of the inadequacy of their message and methods. (The societal challenges will make it as obvious
as tar on snow!) I personally believe in the full gospel, not just
speaking in tongues and falling under the power, but the whole
gospel for the whole man to the whole community that impacts the
whole city and nation!

In conclusion, I say again, Isn't this where all this united, strategic prayer movement is headed? Do you believe God answers prayer? Do you believe God has led the body of Christ nationally to be involved in Concerts of Prayer, Marches for Jesus, prayer walks and spiritual mapping? What is the purpose of all this except that Christianity should influence every level of society? In other words, the goal of the various unity movements is the lordship of Christ over every aspect of our land! This is none other than the incarnation of the kingdom of God. It's an answer to how Jesus told us to pray in Luke 11:2: "And he said unto them, when ye pray, say, Our Father which art in heaven, Hallowed be thy name. Thy kingdom come. Thy will be done, as in heaven, so in earth." This, I believe, will be brought in by the next wave, which will be a true apostolic reformation!

CHAPTER 12

THE COMING APOSTOLIC REFORMATION

The term *fivefold ministry* is just an easier way of saying all the ministry gifts mentioned in Ephesians 4:11 (apostles, prophets, pastors, teachers, evangelists). While much has been said and tremendous light has been placed on this subject, there is still a limitation put on these ministry gifts as a result of the "ghetto mentality" of the church. Let's begin by examining Ephesians 4:7–11.

The Purpose of Fivefold Ministry

But unto every one of us is given grace according to the measure of the gift of Christ. Wherefore he saith, When he ascended up on high, he led captivity captive, and gave gifts unto men. (Now that he ascended, what is it but that he also descended first into the lower parts of the earth? He that descended is the same also that ascended up far above all heavens, that he might fill all things.) And he gave some, apostles; and some, prophets; and some, evangelists; and some, pastors and teachers.
—EPHESIANS 4:7–11

Verse 7 tells us that we receive grace according to the measure of the gift of Christ. Since we all want God's grace, then it must be important for us to find out what this "gift of Christ is"! Verse 8 then tells us that when Christ ascended into heaven, He gave "gifts" unto men.

So now we know two things:

1.   God's grace is given through a certain "gift" of Christ.

2.   These gifts were given when He ascended on high.

Let's find out what these gifts that dispense God's grace are. Verse 11 has the answer. These gifts that impart God's grace are apostles, prophets, pastors, teachers and evangelists. For those of you who don't think going to church is important, I know what you just read came as a shock to you! The Bible not only commands us to fellowship in a church (Heb. 10:25), but it also actually tells us in this passage that unless we are sitting under true fivefold ministry (for preaching, teaching, discipling, vision, strategy, proper government and biblical concepts), we will be missing out on the grace of God we need in life!

Someone might ask, "Are you telling me that I can't go to heaven unless fivefold ministry influences me? I thought the Bible teaches me in Ephesians 2:8–9, 'For by grace are ye saved through faith; and that not of yourselves: it is the gift of God: Not of works, lest any man should boast,' that I am saved by grace through faith."

Wait a minute here! I'm not talking about going to heaven! By reading Ephesians 4:12—"For the perfecting of the saints, for the work of the ministry, for the edifying of the body of Christ"—you see that the grace imparted by fivefold ministry is not saving grace but grace that matures us and properly equips us for the work of the ministry. Reading a gospel tract can save anybody. But true kingdom maturity that qualifies you to be strong enough to save and empower others comes from God working through fivefold ministry.

Furthermore, the amount of grace you receive depends totally on how "much" a "measure" of grace that particular ministry gift has. (Not all fivefold ministry gifts have fully matured or reached their potential either!) Actually there may be someone who qualifies as an apostle in one region or in one country; in another region the ministry giftings and measure of grace they have is much deeper, and so, in comparison, they may not measure up to the regional standard of an apostle. It's even possible that some prophets and teachers may have more apostolic understanding and greater apostolic anointing (because all apostolic men reproduce apostolic anointing in other ministry gifts) than other regions' top apostles!

The Fullness of Christ

When will the fivefold ministry gifts be unnecessary?

> Till we all come in the unity of the faith, and of the knowledge of the Son of God, unto a perfect man, unto the measure of the stature of the fulness of Christ.
>
> —EPHESIANS 4:13

Obviously this verse shows that we still have need of fivefold

ministry function; this need for fivefold ministry will continue
until we come into the fullness of Christ. What is meant by "the
fullness of Christ"? To understand this, let's go back to Ephesians
1:9–11:

> Having made known unto us the mystery of his will,
> according to his good pleasure which he hath purposed in
> himself: That in the dispensation of the fulness of times he
> might gather together in one all things in Christ, both
> which are in heaven, and which are on earth; even in him:
> In whom also we have obtained an inheritance, being pre-
> destinated according to the purpose of him who worketh
> all things after the counsel of his own will.

Many believers are constantly wondering what the will of God
is. Let me just propose here that you cannot begin to know your
own destiny or even write out a personal mission statement until
you know God's mission for the cross!

Therein again, to repeat something spoken in an earlier chapter,
Jesus didn't die on the cross just so that you can go to heaven, but
so He can establish His kingdom on Planet Earth. This is further
elaborated in these verses. Verse 9 tells us that God has revealed the
mystery of His will (God's mission shouldn't be a mystery anymore). His will, it further says, was based according to His intrin-
sic (self-motivated) purpose. What is this purpose? That in the
administration (what God's ultimate goal is, where He's heading
toward) of the fullness (there is that word again) of time He might
gather together in one all things in Christ, both which are in
heaven and which are on earth. There it is—this is what Ephesians
4:13 is talking about! This is why God gave us apostles, prophets,
pastors, teachers and evangelists. Gods' ultimate, ultimate is not
that He would use fivefold ministry just to save souls, but to gather
together in one all *things* in Christ! Things—not just souls, not just
in heaven—but things on earth! Remember that the psalmist wrote
that the earth is the Lord's and the fullness (there's that word *fullness* again) thereof (Ps. 24:1).

When Jesus was crowned Lord of all, it was over God's entire
jurisdiction—not just the church—and this includes all "things."
All "things" include the land, the environment, politics, education,
science, medicine, healthcare, the arts, space, economics, social
justice and all the humanities. "In Christ" means that earth and

heaven will be totally in harmony—both aligned under the leadership of Christ; that's when we will experience the measure of the stature of the fullness of Christ!

> That at the name of Jesus every knee should bow, of things
> in heaven, and things in earth, and things under the earth.
> —Philippians 2:10

All "things" should bow to the lordship of Christ—not just human beings. (Because God delegated Planet Earth to humankind, then when man submits to Christ all "things" under His care will follow anyway.)

The pagans shouldn't be leading the way in science, education, logic, the humanities, law and the environment. The church should be leading the way, influencing the whole world—all the people and all the resources of the world should be under the lordship of Christ. Then and only then will the leading experts have the proper balance and have the right answers with which to tackle all the grave concerns we have politically, socially, economically and environmentally on the planet.

Because the church has been ghettoized to only the ecclesiastical portion of the planet, we have scientists making great technological advances without the restraints and guidelines of godly ethics (for example, the ethics of cloning). Instead, evolution scientists have become society's conscience as sort of naturalistic priests, even interpreting all reality through naturalistic philosophy. The results will be disastrous in the next generation if the church doesn't repent and embrace the "all things" goal of the cross!

Who Will Carry Out This Plan of God?

> Which he wrought in Christ, when he raised him from the
> dead, and set him at his own right hand in the heavenly
> places, far above all principality, and power, and might, and
> dominion, and every name that is named, not only in this
> world, but also in that which is to come: And hath put all
> things under his feet, and gave him to be the head over all
> things to the church, which is his body, the fulness of him
> that filleth all in all.
> —Ephesians 1:20–23

When Jesus rose from the dead, He put all "things" under His feet and became the head of the church, which is His body, *the fullness of Him that fills all in all!*

The church is the earthly fullness of Him who fills all in all! According to this verse, God has plans for the church to be the ones who fill all "things" and reconcile all things under the lordship of Christ. We are His official agents of change that will eventually use the powerful message of the gospel of the kingdom of God to subsume all the cultures under His rule and reign! Hallelujah!

In conclusion to this chapter, let's read Ephesians 4:10: "He that descended is the same also that ascended up far above all heavens, that he might fill all things." This verse tells us that Jesus ascended into heaven so that He will *"fill all things."*

The very next verse says, "And he gave some, apostles; and some, prophets; and some, evangelists; and some, pastors and teachers." This tells us who will lead and equip the church so that Jesus is Lord over every aspect of life so He can "fill all things," not just in heaven but on earth!

This gives further light now on the proper interpretation of Ephesians 4:12. Fivefold ministry is obviously not just called to disciple and empower people to be ecclesiastical preachers and ministers. It is to set up the church and even focus ministry on equipping people to fill up all things. The purpose of Ephesians 4:11 (fivefold ministry) is found in Ephesians 4:10, "that he might fill all things."

A big mistake many pastors make is trying to take everybody with leadership potential aside and make them another preacher! Some aren't called to preach—even though they are called to lead. One of the results of the church waking up as to the gospel of the kingdom will be that the church will be the training center of not only pastors, elders, deacons, ushers and Sunday school workers. The church will also begin to train and empower future politicians, doctors, lawyers, judges, social workers, educators, apologists and economists (so "He can fill all things").

The coming apostolic reformation should result in placing godly leadership in every facet of society with a biblical world-view. Right now we are losing some of our best leaders to secular politics, universities and corporations because there is no room for them in the current church leadership if they don't feel called to preach! We are losing some of the smartest people in the world to dead humanistic philosophies because many intellectuals are looking for a philosophy with answers that harmonize all of life out of one matrix. Instead they see a church that is only able to offer us answers in the spiritual world—in the sweet by and by!

I propose that if someone is truly apostolic, then they already have the wisdom, strategy and grace to disciple and raise up people who can lead corporations as CEOs, entrepreneurs and even heads of communities, states and nations (depending on the measure of their grace)!

Pastors should not only build community within their church by pushing cell groups; they should also be the patriarchs of whole communities! Teachers should not only train future Sunday school workers and lay ministers, but also indoctrinate future medical doctors (who refuse to perform abortions), lawyers and university professors with a biblical world-view. Evangelists will recruit thousands not just to go to heaven but who also are able to "see the kingdom" and be converted into the kingdom army to be disciples and fill all things!

Some apostles and prophets will not just plant and build churches, but they will have the structures for managing and rebuilding ruined cities and nations. If angels can learn from the church, so can the world!

> To the intent that now unto the principalities and powers in heavenly places might be known by the church the manifold wisdom of God.
>
> —EPHESIANS 3:10

We need apostles speaking into kings and presidents (not just to pastors), prophets serving in presidential cabinets, teachers structuring nations' educational policies. Do you get the picture? Our Bible schools should not only give potential leaders a choice in being trained in theology, homiletics and church history, but also have electives in business management, logic, kingdom economics, political science, law, world history and science—all with a biblical kingdom slant. (I believe that all Bible schools should be under the direction of fivefold ministry and in harmony with the local church.) Parents and Sunday schools should give their children a biblical world-view to counter the pagan world-view with which they are constantly being indoctrinated! Telling nice Bible stories that are disconnected to God's ultimate purpose of Christianizing the world won't cut it anymore! When our children are confronted with pagan world-views that encompass all of life, they had better be ready for it (or we can lose them to the world). We need to especially go after high school and college age students and teach them a biblical world-view so that they can properly interpret their education and be trained for kingdom leadership. (I thank God for Dr. David Noebel who has been doing this very thing the last three decades in Summit Ministries.)

We desperately need to train qualified biblical leadership to be ready to step in at the God-ordained moment after revival hits our cities, or the effects of our coming revival will never last! If we don't do this now, then we will only be preparing the next generation for a new wine with a decade-old wineskin that can't sustain the next reformation!

Tertullian, the great North African lawyer, taunted the Roman Empire with these words: "We [the church] are but of yesterday, but we have filled every place among you—cities, islands, fortresses, towns, market places, the very camp, tribes, companies, palace, senate, forum—we have left nothing to you but the temples of your gods."[1]

To quote Dr. Ray Bakke, "Early Christians penetrated the whole city, but not by merely claiming space for church buildings or programs of their own. They penetrated everybody else's instead!"[2]

CHAPTER 13

TEN THINGS ABOUT THE
GOSPEL OF THE KINGDOM

1. It Includes All Truth

Francis Schaeffer said, "When I say Christianity is truth I mean it is true to total reality—the total of what is, beginning with the central reality, the objective existence of the personal-infinite God." [1]

John 18:37 tells us of an exchange between the Lord Jesus and Pilate:

> Pilate therefore said unto him, Art thou a king then? Jesus answered, Thou sayest that I am a king. To this end was I born, and for this cause came I into the world, that I should bear witness unto the truth. Every one that is of the truth heareth my voice.

The God who created the universe also made absolute physical laws (what the science of physics is all about), moral laws (what the laws of sowing and reaping are all about) and spiritual law. (The dietary laws of the Book of Leviticus alone can prove the inspiration of the Bible.) Jesus said, "My words are spirit, and they are life." (See John 6:63.)

Romans 8:2 talks about the law of the spirit. This has to do with yielding to either the Holy Spirit or another spirit. (Which spirit empowers you?) This is the authority you have behind your life and your words.

> If ye abide in me, and my words abide in you, ye shall ask what ye will, and it shall be done unto you.
>
> —JOHN 15:7

Spiritual law also includes principles of spiritual impartation, gifts of healing and miracles and the revelatory gifts.

The same God who inspired John 3:16 also put into place absolute natural laws such as certain chemical interactions that result in gases and water, and even the law of gravity and the law of lift that transcends the law of gravity. The greatest scientists of old dedicated themselves to studying the natural universe because they wanted to know more about God and His wonderful works.

> The works of the LORD are great, sought out of all them that
> have pleasure therein.
>
> —PSALM 111:2

> The heavens declare the glory of God; and the firmament
> sheweth his handywork. Day unto today uttereth speech,
> and night unto night sheweth knowledge. There is no
> speech nor language, where their voice is not heard.
>
> —PSALM 19:1–3

Few people realize that perhaps the greatest scientist in all history, Isaac Newton, wrote more books on theology than he did on science. Though he was off doctrinally (he was an Arian Christian), his belief that the universe was divinely designed led him to believe that the universe was founded with fixed, ordered laws that can be discovered and understood. This led him to discover calculus and other things, like the laws of motion.

Christianity embraces a comprehensive view that marshals history, philosophy, natural, spiritual and moral law, economics, sociology, politics, the arts, literature, healthcare, diet and science toward the glory of God and the lordship of Christ! You can only understand the true purpose and ideals of each of these subjects through the lens of Scripture and by the illumination of the Holy Spirit. Thank God that in the future our sons and daughters will be able to get degrees in these subjects without hurting their faith in God's Word!

The effects of Darwinism

As a side note, many Christians focus all their efforts in fighting certain causes, whether it is abortion, pornography, racism or destruction of the family. What most don't realize is that the main underpinning behind all of the main cultural issues against Christianity today is the theory of evolution! When Charles Darwin's *Origin of Species* was published in 1859, it caused an anti-God tidal wave that is still being felt today. Why? If you do away with God, you do away with the Bible. If you do away with the Bible, you do away with all moral, ethical and cultural standards and absolutes! If you have no creator, then human life is no more important than that of a cat or a dog; your great-grandfather is a one-celled amoeba and your cousin is a maple tree! That leads the way for abortion (because human life isn't special; it isn't any more important than that of an animal because we are all the same). It leads to a New Age pantheism (the belief that everything is God) because it means that we are related to everything in the universe—whether animate or inanimate objects. It leads to moral relativism (because the Ten Commandments and all written creeds and historic documents are all outdated in the present progress of enlightenment on our evolutionary path). It also leads to racism because ethnic supremacists can all believe that their race is the most maturely evolved up the evolutionary ladder (like Adolph Hitler with his view on the Aryan Race).

What we need more than anything else in our educational systems is academically trained creationists who will challenge this hellish theory! (Evolution is more like a natural philosophy than scientific fact.)

So you can see that if Christianity doesn't encompass a worldview that includes all of the truth, not just biblical truth (which is the highest form of absolute truth and stands as the ultimate frame of reference for judging all our ideas), then we will never be able to combat these pagan world-views that are continuing to captivate the minds of today's youth via media, school and peer pressure.

Second Corinthians 10:3–5 says:

> For though we walk in the flesh, we do not war after the flesh: (For the weapons of our warfare are not carnal, but mighty through God to the pulling down of strong holds;) casting down imaginations, and every high thing that exalteth itself against the knowledge of God, and bringing into captivity every thought to the obedience of Christ.

This verse is not just about strongholds in individual minds, but strongholds in whole cultures that can be broken with the knowledge of God and our understanding of truth.

2. It Includes All Things

Again we must understand that the purpose of the cross was not only to reconcile men, but also to legally bring the jurisdiction of the planet back under the reign of God. Colossians 1:19–20 tells us:

> For it pleased the Father that in him should all fulness
> dwell; and, having made peace through the blood of his
> cross, by him to reconcile all things unto himself; by him,
> I say, whether they be things in earth, or things in heaven.

Notice the words *fullness* and *things* are spoken of here. God has not only called us back to Himself by the cross, but He has also called us back to our original birthright of stewarding the earth (Gen. 1:26–28). Since the Resurrection, God commanded us to go to all nations and to bring the gospel to all creation (Matt. 28:19–20). Mark 16:15 says, "And he said unto them, Go ye into all the world, and preach the gospel to every creature."

Matthew 28:20 has to do with all people, and Mark 16:15 has to do with the whole of creation. (This doesn't mean we should go to trees and preach the gospel, but that the gospel was meant to bring the earth back to its proper owner and order!)

I heard someone say once that pastors are called not to a local church but to a geographic area. I concur with this. I want to take this thought a step further—we are not only called to a certain geographic area, but we are called to *liberate* a certain geographic area. The church as a whole is called to liberate Planet Earth and present it to King Jesus! Too radical, you say? Let's see what Scripture has to say about land. Let's take a moment to study a theology of the land, or landology.

The cry of Sodom (See also Jonah 1:2)

In Genesis 18 we see three angels coming to bring news of the birth of Isaac the next year, plus they announce the destruction of Sodom and Gomorrah. Let's see how God knew about the sinful state of Sodom.

> And the LORD said, Because the cry of Sodom and
> Gomorrah is great, and because their sin is very grievous; I
> will go down now, and see whether they have done alto-
> gether according to the cry of it, which is come unto me;
> and if not, I will know.
> —GENESIS 18:20–21

Jehovah said it was the "cry of Sodom" that alerted Him. I ask you, What does that mean? Does it mean there were people sobbing there? I think not. Does it mean somebody was crying out the word of the Lord, or crying out to God in prayer? I don't think so. By the biblical account we have of Sodom, it doesn't look as if anyone did much preaching or praying—including Lot!

Then what does it mean? The word *cry* in Genesis 18:20 is *zaaq*, and it means to shriek from anguish or danger. Who was it that shrieked from anguish or danger? Was it Lot? It doesn't seem to me from the biblical account that Lot even had a clue that he was in danger. Besides, Scripture says "the cry of Sodom"; it was some sort of corporate cry! A corporate cry can either come from all the people crying out that they were in danger. (It couldn't be that because if they knew they were in danger they would have moved or changed their behavior). Or it could have come from the geographical land of Sodom. Crazy, you think? Perhaps to our thinking, but what, then, did it mean by the "cry of Sodom...is come unto me"? Who are we to say God didn't create His universe with the capability of somehow communicating with its Maker when things weren't lined up correctly. (Even cars with their built-in computers tell us when something is wrong!) Doesn't Scripture teach that creation responds to God's glory and worships Him?

> For ye shall out with joy, and be led forth with peace: the mountains and the hills shall break forth before you into singing, and all the trees of the field shall clap their hands.
> —ISAIAH 55:12

> The heavens declare the glory of God; and the firmament sheweth his handywork.
> —PSALM 19:1

> Be still, and know that I am God: I will be exalted among the heathen, I will be exalted in the earth.
> —PSALM 46:10

> For every beast of the forest is mine, and the cattle upon a thousand hills. I know all the fowls of the mountains: and the wild beasts of the field are mine.
> —PSALM 50:10–11

> Let the people praise thee, O God; let all the people praise thee. Then shall the earth yield her increase; and God, even our own God, shall bless us.
> —PSALM 67:5–6

The floods have lifted up, O LORD, the floods have lifted up
their voice; the floods lift up their waves.
—PSALM 93:3

Let the heavens rejoice, and let the earth be glad; let the sea
roar, and the fulness thereof. Let the field be joyful, and all
that is therein: then shall all the trees of the wood rejoice.
—PSALM 96:11–12

Let the floods clap their hands, let the hills be joyful
together.
—PSALM 98:8

Didn't Lord Jesus tell the Pharisees that if the people didn't
praise Him, the stones would immediately cry out? (See Luke
19:40.)

I came to the conclusion a long time ago that there are many
things in Scripture that are hard for me to understand, but that
doesn't mean Scripture isn't true. I believe God's Word clearly
teaches us that not only should we believe God for souls, but also
that we have the right as children of God to claim every ounce of
dirt and real estate on the earth for Him! God has given us the
power to get these resources so His covenant with the world can be
established in the earth. (See Deuteronomy 8:18.) God told
Abraham that he and his seed (those who believe in Lord Jesus) are
the heirs of the whole world (which includes the land and everything in it. (See Romans 4:13.) Second Corinthians 5:19 says that
Jesus reconciled *the world* (Greek *kosmos*, the whole created order)
to Himself.

God wants not only the souls of men, but He also wants Planet
Earth delivered back to the jurisdiction of His people so He can
have rule over all things. The earth, not only the world system,
should be brought back under the rule of God. It even cries out for
it! The Bible says in Revelation 11:18 that God will destroy those
who destroy the earth (not necessarily only talking about hurting
the environment by pollution, but by not using the land for its
original intent, thus destroying the purpose of the land).

Scriptures teach us that when sin gets too severe in a certain
geographic area, it so repulses the ground because of its misuse
that the land itself spits them out! (Perhaps this means it refuses to
yield its increase of crops and forces them to leave.) Leviticus

18:20–28 teaches us that because of the sins of killing one's off-spring, adultery, homosexuality and bestiality, the land was defiled and vomited out its inhabitants! In Genesis 4:9–12 we see that God knew that Cain killed Abel because Abel's blood cried out to God from the ground! The sinner defiles the ground (against its created purpose), and it cries out for deliverance!

Numbers 16 shows us that when Korah led a rebellion against Moses, the ground responded to God and swallowed up Korah and his followers alive and sent them to Sheol. In Matthew 10 Jesus tells His disciples to shake the dust off their feet if the gospel isn't received in a city. Evidently not only were the people defiled and in sin, but their disobedience caused the very ground they owned and lived on to be defiled! Paul continued this tradition of shaking the dust off his feet when the leaders of Pisidia Antioch rejected him (Acts 13:51). I guess Paul didn't want a speck of dirt attached to him that was used by those who rejected the rule and jurisdiction of God.

Finally, Romans 8:19–22 says:

> For the earnest expectation of the creature waiteth for the manifestation of the sons of God. For the creature was made subject to vanity, not willingly, but by reason of him who hath subjected the same in hope, because the creature itself also shall be delivered from the bondage of corruption into the glorious liberty of the children of God. For we know that the whole creation groaneth and travaileth in pain together until now.

This teaches us as clear as can be that not only humankind but also all of creation is in vanity (v. 20) because the created order is not being used for God's glory. Verse 22 tells us that creation is in bondage and is eternally groaning (crying out) and travailing in pain until the glorious liberty of the children of God. Creation (the trees, the land, the animal kingdom and the world's resources) is waiting for the manifestation (the unveiling) of the sons of God! Not only are God and the angels waiting and rooting for us, but even the ground we walk on, the highways we drive on and the money we trade with are all crying out to God for the church to wake up and finally come out of the shadows of our church ghettos and to deliver them from defilement and release them for their original intent—the glory of God!

3. The Kingdom Includes
All Gift Ministries

The gospel of the kingdom not only has provided us with fivefold ministry but also elders, deacons and deaconesses, helps, administration and all the different manifestations of the Holy Spirit that fit in perfectly with each person according to their particular calling and training. It all starts in the local church and then should branch out to the whole created order.

The body of Christ is strong right now in its giftings but limited in how and where these giftings should be used. The body of Christ, not the world, should be the experts on how to place people into their giftings, call and vocation. As Luther said, we must serve God in the midst of the world by faithfully performing the tasks of our daily occupations. Shoemakers, housekeepers, farmers and businessmen, if they do their work to the glory of God, are more pleasing to Him than monks and nuns.[2] We should be the leaders in developing ways on how people can know their ministry gifts, strengths, weaknesses, propensities, passions and personality types. All this is so that we know not only how to place people in the church, but also how to help them play out their role in the created order of the kingdom of God.

4. The Gospel of the Kingdom
Is Revealed in History

It is clear from reading Scripture that God deals with mankind through covenants. He is a covenant-keeping God. Just a quick glance through Scripture shows us that God made covenant with Adam, Noah, Abraham, Isaac, Jacob, Moses, David and Solomon; of course, the Lord Jesus made a new covenant with the church. Two of the components of a covenant are ethical stipulations (the agreement of terms of the covenant) and sanctions (the rewards of either keeping the covenant or punishment for not keeping it).

Since God created Adam, the moral laws of sowing and reaping and the laws known in conscience even by people who never heard the gospel are evident. History shows that *just* nations are blessed and *unjust* nations are cursed: for example, World War I and World War II (the survival of Churchill's England and the demise of Hitler), the Civil War (the South lost because it refused to give up on slavery for mostly economic reasons), the U.S. War for Independence (England lost because it was unjustly oppressing the thirteen colonies). The French Revolution failed because of espousing atheistic humanism as its ideal, and most recently, the Soviet Union fell apart (the curse of God was upon them because communism and socialism promote messianic *statism*—the state provides all your needs and tries to abolish faith in God). We can go on and on and on. As I said before, history is His story. It is a lesson in moral philosophy! Only Christianity has an accurate world-view that encompasses all of past, present and future world history! Not only church history, but also world history, shows God is sovereign over all the nations and orders their destiny according to His sovereignty; it is important for saints to understand world history as well as church history.

> Thou, O king, art a king of kings: for the God of heaven hath given thee a kingdom, power, and strength, and glory. And wheresoever the children of men dwell, the beasts of the field and the fowls of the heaven hath he given into thine hand, and hath made thee ruler over them all. Thou art this head of gold. And after thee shall arise another kingdom inferior to thee, and another third kingdom of brass, which shall bear rule over all the earth. And the fourth kingdom shall be strong as iron, forasmuch as iron breaketh in pieces and subdueth all things. And as iron that breaketh all these, shall it break in pieces and bruise. And whereas thou sawest the feet and toes, part of potters' clay, and part of iron, the kingdom shall be divided; but there shall be in it of the strength of the iron, forasmuch as thou sawest the iron mixed with miry clay. And as the toes of the feet were part of iron, and part of clay, so the kingdom shall be partly strong, and partly broken. And whereas thou sawest iron mixed with miry clay, they shall mingle themselves with the seed of men: but they shall not cleave one to another, even as iron is not mixed with clay. And in the days of these kings shall the God of heaven set up a kingdom, which shall never be destroyed: and the kingdom shall not be left to other people, but it shall break in pieces and consume all these kingdoms, and it shall stand for ever.

> —Daniel 2:37–44

And they shall drive thee from men, and thy dwelling shall be with the beasts of the field: they shall make thee to eat grass as oxen, and seven times shall pass over thee, until thou know that the most High ruleth in the kingdom of men, and giveth it to whomsoever he will. The same hour was the thing fulfilled upon Nebuchadnezzar: and he was driven from men, and did eat grass as oxen, and his body was wet with the dew of heaven, till his hairs were grown like eagles' feathers, and his nails like birds' claws. And at the end of the days I Nebuchadnezzar lifted up mine eyes unto heaven, and mine understanding returned unto me, and I blessed the most High, and I praised and honoured him that liveth for ever, whose dominion is an everlasting dominion, and his kingdom is from generation to genera-tion: And all the inhabitants of the earth are reputed as nothing: and he doeth according to his will in the army of heaven, and among the inhabitants of the earth: and none can stay his hand, or say unto him, What doest thou?

—DANIEL 4:32–35

I saw in the night visions, and, behold, one like the Son of man came with the clouds of heaven, and came to the Ancient of days, and they brought him near before him. And there was given him dominion, and glory, and a king-dom, that all people, nations, and languages, should serve him: his dominion is an everlasting dominion, which shall not pass away, and his kingdom that which shall not be destroyed...And the kingdom and dominion, and the greatness of the kingdom under the whole heaven, shall be given to the people of the saints of the most High, whose kingdom is an everlasting kingdom, and all dominions shall serve and obey Him.

—DANIEL 7:13–14, 27

Behold, the nations are as a drop of a bucket, and are counted as the small dust of the balance: behold, he taketh up the isles as a very little thing...All nations before him are as nothing; and they are counted to him less nothing, and vanity...It is he that sitteth upon the circle of the earth, and the inhabitants thereof are as grasshoppers; that stretcheth out the heavens as a curtain, and spreadeth them out as a tent to dwell in: That bringeth the princes to noth-ing; he maketh the judges of the earth as vanity. Yea, they shall not be planted; yea, they shall not be sown: yea, their stock shall not take root in the earth: and he shall also blow upon them, and they shall wither, and the whirlwind shall take them away as stubble.

—ISAIAH 40:15, 17, 22–24

And hath made of one blood all nations of men for to dwell on all the face of the earth, and hath determined the times before appointed, and the bounds of their habitation. That they should seek the Lord, if haply they might feel after him, and find him, though he be not far from every one of us.

—ACTS 17:26–27

When the Most High divided to the nations their inheritance, when he separated the sons of Adam, he set the bounds of the people according to the number of the children of Israel.

—DEUTERONOMY 32:8

By these were the isles of the Gentiles divided in their lands; every one after his tongue, after their families, in their nations.

—GENESIS 10:5

And the LORD came down to see the city and the tower, which the children of men builded. And the LORD said, Behold, the people is one, and they have all one language; and this they begin to do: and now nothing will be restrained from them, which they have imagined to do. Go to, let us go down and there confound their language, that they may not understand one another's speech. So the LORD scattered them abroad from thence upon the face of all the earth: and they left off to build the city.

—GENESIS 11:5–8

We can learn the ways of God from reading world history as well as reading church history. History is merely His story, His plan and His purpose revealed. To study history is to study God in action. Even when Karl Marx wanted to revolutionize the world, the first thing he did was to go after and proselytize the newspaper people. The next thing he did was help rewrite history so he could marginalize and de-emphasize the positive effects of Christianity! We must realize that when people come into the world, they inherit the debits and credits of previous generations.

That's why we need historians that can show a consistent, connecting world-view of history that illustrates the blessings of obeying God's laws and the curses of disobedience for the nations.

Scriptural examples

Second Samuel 21:1–2 says, "Then there was a famine in the days of David three years, year after year; and David inquired of the LORD. And the LORD answered, It is for Saul, and for his bloody house, because he slew the Gibeonites. And the king called the Gibeonites, and said unto them; (now the Gibeonites were not of the children of Israel, but of the remnant of the Amorites; and the children of Israel had sworn unto them: and Saul sought to slay them in his zeal to the children of Israel and Judah.)"

This shows that God sent Israel a famine in the land because the previous king (Saul) shed innocent blood. On the other hand, God preserved Israel during the reign of King Hezekiah because He was showing favor for a previous king's sake (David): "For I will defend this city, to save it, for mine own sake, and for my servant David's sake" (2 Kings 19:34). It is impossible to know why we are in the state we are in now without knowing the past! Because all of history is important to God, we need to know if something that happened in our city's past is stopping God from accomplishing His purposes. Furthermore, it is impossible to know where you are going (and why you are going there) if you don't where you came from!

Building for tomorrow

> Which we have heard and known, and our fathers have told us. We will not hide them from their children, shewing to the generation to come the praises of the LORD, and his strength, and his wonderful works that he hath done. For he established a testimony in Jacob, and appointed a law in Israel, which he commanded our fathers, that they should make them known to their children: That the generation to come might know them, even the children which should be born; who should arise and declare them to their children: That they might set their hope in God, and not forget the works of God, but keep his commandments: And might not be as their fathers, a stubborn and rebellious generation; a generation that set not their heart aright, and whose spirit was not steadfast with God.
>
> —PSALM 78:3–8

In the gospel of the kingdom we are not trying to establish kingdom principles in our cities overnight. In the past we had superstar mentalities, trying to fill stadiums and change the world in one crusade! But God has called us to build inter-generationally. Those afraid the Antichrist is going to soon take over the world rarely build for tomorrow. They neglect to pour into their young people, encourage them to go to school and invest financially for their future, because they believe that the end is coming any day now!

With this dawning of the new millennium, I predict many people are going to be disillusioned with a lot of what's been written about the last days, and people are going to wake up and begin to build for the future! Very few mega-churches remain successful inter-generationally. Usually when "the man" leaves, so do the people.

As the church applies kingdom principles, we will pour into young leaders as never before! Our main attribute will not only be preaching or planting, but parenting! True spiritual leaders are parents first and preachers second because their main goal is to pour into their sons and daughters with the goal that they will outdo their parents!

> Verily, verily, I say unto you, He that believeth on me, the works that I do shall he do also; and greater works than these shall he do; because I go unto my Father.
>
> —John 14:12

> For the promise is unto you, and to your children, and to all that are afar off, even as many as the Lord our God shall call.
>
> —Acts 2:39

Knowing that God is not in a frenzied rush, I know that history shows that the gospel has always overcome all odds! The Roman Empire couldn't crush the church, and the barbaric tribes couldn't stop the church. Neither did the corrupt mother church or the enlightenment of the fifteenth century. And the present postmodern culture will not prevail! As we look back in time during these crucial periods, the church not only survived but also overcame all odds and became victorious.

> For unto us a child is born, unto us a son is given: and the government shall be upon his shoulder: and his name shall be called Wonderful, Counsellor, The mighty God, The

everlasting Father, The Prince of Peace. Of the increase of his government and peace there shall be no end, upon the throne of David, and upon his kingdom, to order it, and to establish it with judgment and with justice from henceforth even forever. The zeal of the LORD of hosts will perform this.
—ISAIAH 9:6–7

In conclusion, let's not just build big but build qualitatively a proper foundation that those who come after us can build upon! Let's stop this self-centered superstar mentality that leaves our seed a sloppy mess that they can't build upon because it was built to attract crowds (from other churches) instead of to build the kingdom. (It's very possible to build a "mom and pop" mega-church where the real leadership team only consists of a husband and wife.) Many churches add many members but literally diminish the kingdom in their area because their church growth primarily comes from attracting sheep from smaller, less attractive "feeder" churches. That kind of mega-church has at best a cycle of up and down crowds every three or four years and is rarely successful beyond ten years—never mind inter-generationally! Let's begin to build apostolically!

5. The Kingdom Transcends All Cultures

Many people who pastor churches were taught in the past to only try to reach people who looked like them. Their ministry was more autobiographical than apostolic! They set out to build churches that were homogenous (all the same kind of people). Contrary to many present church growth philosophies, God told us that our mission should be to reflect heaven on earth (Luke 11:2). In heaven, people of all nations, tribes, people and tongues stand before God and worship (Rev. 7:9).

It's one thing to pastor a church in a community that has people of only one ethnic or economic background and your church homogeneously reflects your community. It's quite another thing if your church is in the midst of an integrated neighborhood and your target group is only people who look like you!

The model church was Antioch (Acts 11, 13)

The Antioch church was more of a model apostolic church than the original church in Jerusalem for a number of reasons. One of the main reasons was that their church was able to cross racial lines. The city of Antioch was divided into Greek, Syrian, Jewish, Latin and African sectors. The people used to climb the walls that separated the city racially just to attend church! Believers were first called Christians in Antioch because previously the church was primarily Jewish—so the church looked like another Jewish sect to the world. When the world saw the multi-racial leadership team of Antioch and the multi-racial church community, they didn't know what to call them anymore, so they called them Christians (Acts 11:26).

We have to make a distinction here between racial reconciliation, multi-ethnic churches and multiculturalism. I believe in the former two but not in the latter. The basic definition of culture is a people who share the same race, language, dress, customs, foods and religion. True multiculturalism actually espouses moral relativism because it respects all religious beliefs and discourages proselytizing people to change. Multi-culturalism leads to polytheism (belief in many gods). Polytheism leads to moral relativism (no right or wrong), moral relativism leads to anarchy and chaos, and chaos leads to a totalitarian society! If our churches really became multicultural, then we would all have different beliefs, and very few people would understand one another because there would be no common language. The apostolic model is multi-ethnic but not multicultural!

I believe in multiculturalism as long as it goes no further than respecting and enjoying the different ethnic foods, dress and some harmless customs. Beyond that it's harmful! (Talk about an unsung hero—how about Noah as an example of leading a diverse group. His ark of salvation included a multibiological crew for a year.) Here's an interesting statistic. In 1900, 80 percent of all Christians were white. By 1980 most saints were non-white, non-northern and non-Western.[3]

The bottom line is this: If our gospel only works in nice middle-class suburbs where everyone looks the same, it is not a kingdom gospel! If Christians only want to fellowship within their comfort zone—they truly are not mature believers.

My snapshot

I have been pastoring a church in a poor Hispanic area in the Sunset Park area of Brooklyn, New York since 1984. I started ministering there in full-time ministry in 1980. Through miraculous means we had the opportunity to buy a tremendous facility! We were renting the first thirteen and one-half years of our existence. Many people said we couldn't possibly afford it! (Up until recently only two members—including myself—owned their own home, and only a handful of the working people made even lower-middle-class income.)

When we first started, and up until the early 1990s, almost half the church was on welfare, and a large percentage were single moms. Now, because there is a lift to the gospel, very few people are still on welfare (even including the single mothers)! Furthermore, many people are buying homes and getting promoted to good paying jobs. Though facing insurmountable odds, after almost one year of negotiating and looking for a mortgage, our church was able to bring in during the year of 1997, an average of more than $6,000 per working adult in our church! We are experiencing an urban renewal mostly of core young people, many of whom are going to college and have goals of postgraduate degrees! I have a goal of at least ten getting masters' degrees so we can open up a Christian high school with a kingdom world-view of placing leaders in all levels of society.

Why is this happening to us? Because we are preaching the gospel of the kingdom of God, and we are seeing God promote us so that we can begin to take dominion in our community! If our gospel can't work in the worst slum in a Third World country, then we have no right to preach it!

> And they that shall be of thee shall build the old waste places: thou shalt raise up the foundations of many generations; and thou shalt be called, The repairer of the breach, The restorer of paths to dwell in.
>
> —Isaiah 58:12

6. The Kingdom Administrates and Unites All Things

Having made known unto us the mystery of his will, according to his good pleasure which he hath purposed in himself: That in the dispensation of the fulness of times he might gather together in one all things in Christ, both which are in heaven, and which are on earth; even in him: In whom also we have obtained an inheritance, being predestinated

according to the purpose of him who worketh all things after
the counsel of his own will.

—EPHESIANS 1:9–11

Those who have a heart just to build their own empires remain
as islands to themselves! Those who have a heart to reach a city for
Lord Jesus and build the kingdom of God automatically open
themselves up to unite with others because they know that the
kingdom mission is beyond any one church, ministry or minister.

As previously stated, God's goal according to Ephesians 1:9–11
is that in the fullness of times, He might gather together in one all
things in Christ. According to verses 9–10, this is not only His will
and purpose, but it is the only real thing He tries to administrate!
Many pastors are frustrated because they don't believe God is blessing *their work*. That's the problem (*their work*)! The key is we have
to recognize what God is administrating and planning for and just
get behind that and work for it. That's how we get the blessing of
God!

A sign of true apostolic and prophetic people is that they are
"out of themselves" so to speak and recognize this grandiose plan
God is orchestrating right before their eyes. It's no accident that the
last decade experienced global Marches for Jesus, national
Concerts of Prayer, united prayer walks, whole communities doing
spiritual mapping, and citywide compassionate ministry. God is up
to something, something bigger than just one local church or one
para-church ministry. In this plan there are no superstars except
the Lord Jesus. In order for God to now take it beyond the unity
movement and the prayer and march movement, we need apostolic
and prophetic people to lead us into what God has been working
toward since Adam's sin—the gathering together in one of all
things under the lordship of Christ!

People are getting excited over unity, and that's good. People are
getting excited over prayer, and that's good. But unless we take it
to the next level and begin to see an incarnation of that for which
we are believing, unless we see apostolic leaders unite together
with other apostolic leaders, apostolic streams and networks with
networks—leading us to a kingdom reformation—we have not yet
seen that which God is really going after! Perhaps we will never see
it, but if we build correctly and obey God, maybe our grandchil-
dren will see it!

The body of Christ in the 1970s saw the emphasis of mega-churches; the 1980s saw the emphasis of apostolic streams and networks; the 1990s are seeing the network of networks. I hope that in the new millennium the world will begin to see the reality of the incarnation of the kingdom of God (as a result of all this unity). Even so, come, Lord Jesus.

7. The Kingdom Produces Heroes

One of the things the world does to frame its particular world-view is to "media-ize" those they want to prop up as heroes. The world skillfully presents to our children those that represent their world-view as someone to emulate. In recent times people such as Gianni Versace, the murdered fashion designer, got front-page coverage for weeks even though he lived a selfish, sensual, homosexual lifestyle. This lifestyle featured scantily clad men hired as servants waiting on him and his guests in his posh beachfront house in Miami, Florida. But when Mother Theresa died, she barely got important coverage for a week, and mostly it was not front-page news. (It's not a coincidence that she was a strong Pro-Life advocate.) This is a not-so-subtle way for biased news reporters to attempt to indoctrinate the masses as to what and who is really important (and news worthy)! In most Christian homes I would guess the walls of our children would be adorned with the latest sports or music stars (although some of these people are OK). There is an imbalance here!

The greatest heroes in the history of this planet have been people with a biblical world-view. We cannot depend on the media or the school systems to accurately portray history or even heroes of the faith. Our children need to be soaked, not only with stories of courage, valor and integrity from people like David, Deborah, Moses, Joseph, Daniel, Jeremiah, Peter and Paul, but we need to make our children aware of heroes throughout history. One of the greatest bedtime stories for children used by John Calvin was *Fox's Book of Martyrs*. (Now, with the revised version written in modern English, this is a must for your children to read.)

Our children need to know the stories of martyrs like Polycarp, Ignatius and Justin (early church fathers); in the Middle Ages, people like Joan of Arc, John Hus and John Wycliffe; during the Renaissance, men like Martin Luther, Zwingli and Calvin; and in

American history, people like Christopher Columbus (who was guided to the New World by the Holy Spirit), Pocahontas (the true story of her conversion to Christianity and her heroism), George Whitefield, Patrick Henry, William Wilberforce and Charles Finney; and in more recent times, people like Teddy Roosevelt, William (Daddy) Seymour, Dietrich Bonhoffer, Billy Graham, Winston Churchill, Dr. Martin Luther King Jr., Frances Schaeffer and Mother Teresa. All these were people of principles and uncommon courage. They were people willing to face all odds and still hold to their God-appointed destiny. We must teach our children (contrary to the hedonistic, pleasure-centered American media culture we see now) that life is not worth living if it's not worth dying for something!

> And they overcame him by the blood of the Lamb, and by the word of their testimony; and they loved not their lives unto the death.
>
> —Revelation 12:11

In closing, let's not forget the real heroes we see today (including faithful fathers and mothers). Point out to your children and describe some of the Christian heroes alive today. They are too numerous to mention here. Don't just show them people in the pastorate, but show them politicians, entrepreneurs, scientists, lawyers and judges who hold up the Christian banner. Thank God we have a lot to choose from simply because the kingdom of God produces the greatest people on earth!

8. It Must Produce Servants

If we want to not only affect but also infect the earth, we have to produce servants! I heard about a pastor recently that grew his church to about five thousand because he decided to mobilize his church to serve its community.

The early church grew by having a servant's heart, imitating their Lord who washed the feet of His disciples. If the early church had ignored the needs of the hungry widows in Acts 6:1, they would have never experienced the revival of Acts 6:7. To quote again from Dr. Ray Bakke:

> Instead of evading the ugly reality of their time—the early church embraced them; by doing what the pagans around

them avoided, they overcame the forces that threatened them! The early church visited the sick and orphans, fed the hungry and took in the outcasts.

This is how Christianity spread in Egypt in the second century—the Christian women working together formed a team. Some went into the streets and collected abandoned babies while other woman nursed the babies. The Christians also collected abandoned rotting corpses in the garbage dumps and gave them a proper burial.

Benedict (A.D. 529) started a monastery organized around a 24-hour day of 6 hours of work, 6 hours of worship, 6 hours of study and 6 hours of sleep. He organized lay people and sent them into the worst, most violent places in Europe. They converted Europe and developed economics and communities in the worst neighborhoods of Europe.[4]

The church will spread the gospel by serving humanity—not by lording it over humanity. (In the early church you were known as a Christian not just by your witnessing but also by your works of charity.)

The gospel is not to spread by the sword but by servanthood. In our nation's history Christians have produced the finest schools (like Harvard, Yale, Princeton and Columbia) and hospitals, abolished slavery and initiated child labor reform and women's rights. This is why our nation is blessed today! Let's continue to keep up the great work.

9. It Is First Won in the Spirit

The gospel of the kingdom is not primarily won in the natural through political processes; it is first won in the spirit through dealing with political (hierarchal) principalities and powers. Before you can displace ungodly rulers in the natural world, you need to first displace ungodly rulers in the spirit world. We must first cast down vain imaginations in the spirit before we can change the pagan world-view in the natural.

Jesus said in Luke 17:21 that the kingdom of God is first seen or experienced in the heart: "Neither shall they say, Lo here! or, lo there! for, behold, the kingdom of God is within you."

And John 3:3–6 says:

> Jesus answered and said unto him, Verily, verily, I say unto
> thee, Except a man be born again, he cannot see the king-
> dom of God. Nicodemus saith unto him, How can a man be
> born when he is old? can he enter the second time into his
> mother's womb, and be born? Jesus answered, Verily, verily,
> I say unto thee, Except a man be born of water and of the
> Spirit, he cannot enter into the kingdom of God. That
> which is born of the flesh is flesh; and that which is born
> of Spirit is spirit.

God builds His kingdom and speaks to mankind from the inside
and then works to the outside world. How do we expect to drive
ruling demons from city hall if we can't control our own passions
and lust? (Internal integrity results in external integration.) The
strategy of the devil is the opposite of God's. He wants us to work
on the outside before the inside is changed.

We can see how the strategy of the enemy works by the strategies of the Marxists. Taking their cue from Karl Marx's *Communist
Manifesto*, communists believe that the environment is to blame for
the ills of society. By overthrowing oppressive capitalistic govern-
ments and by the process of redistributing the wealth of a nation
(so that every body is virtually on the same economic level), they
believe it will usher in a utopian (paradise) society that will cure
all the corporate and individual needs of man. Of course, we have
all seen firsthand how far that ideology has taken communism.
(Those communist countries that are still together are among the
poorest and least technologically advanced countries in the world.)

Even today it is popular to blame our surroundings for all our
ills. Environmental determinism (my neighborhood, community
and my atmosphere determine my destiny), psychological determinism (how my parents brought me up) and genetic determinism
(I am the way I am because of my genetic makeup) are all philosophies that have permeated our society. Although there is some
measure of truth in each of those deterministic ideas, God's Word
puts the main emphasis on the personal choices we make in allow-
ing God to deal with our hearts and minds and then dealing with
the spiritual forces of wickedness in a community.

> For this is the covenant that I will make with the house of
> Israel after those days, saith the Lord; I will put *my laws
> into their mind*, and *write them in their hearts*: and I will be

to them a God, and they shall be to me a people. [First is
the internal working of God's Spirit, then the corporate
external effects.]
—HEBREWS 8:10, EMPHASIS ADDED

Wherein in time past ye walked according to the *course of
this world*, according to the *prince of the power of the air*, the
spirit that now worketh in the children of disobedience.
—EPHESIANS 2:2, EMPHASIS ADDED

For we wrestle not against flesh and blood, *but against principalities*, against *powers*, against the rulers of the darkness
of this world, *against spiritual wickedness* in *high places.*
—EPHESIANS 6:12, EMPHASIS ADDED

The greatest sign of spiritual advance and that the strongholds
of hell are being broken in your community is that there is unity in
the body of Christ! If your community doesn't have Spirit-filled
and Holy Spirit–controlled apostolic leadership who are gathering
the body of Christ together to take your community...if there isn't
a spirit of unity and brokenness amongst the spiritual leadership in
your community...then that means there's probably a spirit of
independence, competition, indifference and maybe even old
wounds and animosities that need to be dealt with among pastors
and churches. That geographic area has major satanic strongholds
holding it down, and you must gather together intercessors immediately to pray against division and "believe God" that all those
walls will be brought down!

Behold, how good and how pleasant it is for brethren to
dwell together in unity! It is *like the precious ointment upon
the head*, that ran down upon the beard, even Aaron's beard:
that went down to the skirts of his garments; as the dew of
Hermon, and as the dew that descended upon the moun-
tains of Zion: *for there the* LORD *commanded the blessing,
even life for evermore.*
—PSALM 133:1–3, EMPHASIS ADDED

And Jesus knew their thoughts, and said unto them, *Every
kingdom* divided *against itself is brought to desolation*; and
every city or house divided against itself shall not stand.
—MATTHEW 12:25, EMPHASIS ADDED

Prayer only works if you're in vertical harmony with God and horizontal unity with man. The apostle Peter wrote, "Likewise, ye husbands, dwell with them according to knowledge, giving honour unto the wife, as unto the weaker vessel, and as being heirs together of the grace of life; *that your prayers be not hindered*" (1 Pet. 3:7, emphasis added).

> Therefore I say unto you, What things soever ye desire, when ye pray, believe that ye receive them, and ye shall have them. And *when ye stand praying, forgive*, if you have *ought against any*: that *your Father* also which *is in heaven may forgive* you your *trespasses*.
> —MARK 11:24–25, EMPHASIS ADDED

> Therefore if thou bring thy gift to the altar, and there rememberest that thy brother hath ought against thee; leave there thy gift before the altar, and go thy way; first be reconciled to thy brother, and then come and offer thy gift.
> —MATTHEW 5:23–24

The result of having vertical and horizontal harmony in the body of Christ is that the power of God is released for a whole region!

> These all continued with one accord in prayer and supplication, with the women, and Mary the mother of Jesus, and with his brethren.
> —ACTS 1:14

> And they were all filled with the Holy Ghost, and began to speak with other tongues, as the Spirit gave them utterance.
> —ACTS 2:4

> Then they that gladly received his word were baptized: and the same day there were added unto them about three thousand souls. And they continued steadfastly in the apostles' doctrine and fellowship, and in breaking of bread, and in prayers. And fear came upon every soul: and many wonders and signs were done by the apostles. And all that believed were together, and had all things common.
> —ACTS 2:41–44

> And the multitude of them that believed were of one heart and of one soul: neither said any of them that aught of the things which he possessed was his own; but they had all things in common. And *with great power gave the apostles*

witness of the resurrection of the Lord Jesus: and great grace
was upon them all.
—ACTS 4:32–33, EMPHASIS ADDED

The result of the stronghold of pride and independence broken down among believers is phenomenal! When there is a clean heart between God and man, the windows of heaven are opened and the kingdom of God is demonstrated through signs and wonders! Hebrews 2:3–4 says, "How shall we escape, if we neglect so great salvation; which at the first began to be spoken by the Lord, and was confirmed unto us by them that heard him; God also bearing them witness, both with signs and wonders, and with divers miracles, and gifts of the Holy Ghost, according to his own will?"

> But if I cast out devils by the Spirit of God, then the kingdom of God is come unto you.
> —MATTHEW 12:28

Sometimes it's not that people aren't exercising their faith or reading their Bibles. Sometimes the lack of power in a church is because of a lack of corporate unity in a church or even in a community! (It was because of corporate division in the Corinthian church that many individual believers couldn't get healed! First Corinthians 11:17–18, 21, 30 says, "Now in this that I declare unto you I praise you not, that ye come together not for the better, but for the worse. For first of all, when ye come together in the church, I hear that there be divisions among you; and I partly believe it… For in eating every one taketh before other his own supper: and one is hungry, and another is drunken…For this cause many are weak and sickly among you, and many sleep.")

As God's people unite in love and join their faith together in prayer, the gospel of the kingdom of God will strike down demonic hosts and advertise the gospel with mighty power. Then we can take the political, educational, sociological and natural systems of our community.

10. It Fills All Things

And hath put *all things* under his feet, and gave him to be the head over *all things* to the church, which is his body, *the fulness of him* that *filleth all in all.*
—EPHESIANS 1:22–23, EMPHASIS ADDED

He that descended is the same also that ascended up far above all heavens, that he might *fill all things*.

—Ephesians 4:10, emphasis added

For by him were *all things* created, that are in heaven, and that are in earth, visible and invisible, whether they be thrones, or dominions, or principalities, or powers: *all things* were created by him, and *for him*: And he is before all things, and *by him all things consist*. And he is the head of the body, the church: who is the beginning, the firstborn from the dead; that *in all things he might have the preeminence*. For it pleased the Father that *in him should all fulness dwell*; and, having made peace through the blood of his cross, by him to *reconcile all things unto himself*; by him, I say, whether they *be things in earth*, or things in heaven.

—Colossians 1:16–20, emphasis added

God's will is that Christians permeate every level of society. The monastic movement in the sixth century caused saints to run from the world and pursue a life of holiness and seclusion. The results of this were disastrous! We became irrelevant in much of society and eventually lost ten thousand urban churches in North Africa to Islam. The same pattern of running from the cities is *still taking place* at an alarming rate! While Islam is targeting the cities of America and is the fastest growing urban religion today, more and more Christians are fleeing the cities to pursue a non-threatening life of comfort and ease! My observation through viewing advertisements and personal travel is that a large percentage of American mega-churches are outside the city proper.[5] I also believe that most evangelicals and their Bible schools are also in the suburbs.[6] Unless we repent as a body and begin to target our cities, America will continue to decline. In 1900, 8 percent of the world's population lived in cities. By the year 2000, that number is nearly 50 percent.[7]

God called us (the church) a city on a hill, the light and the salt of the earth (Matt. 5:13–16). Salt was rubbed into foods before refrigeration was utilized, and as it worked its way down to the core of the food, it acted as a preservative. God has called the body of Christ to be yeast that keeps on proliferating and multiplying until it works its way through the whole batch of dough.

> Another parable spake he unto them; The kingdom of
> heaven is like unto leaven, which a woman took, and hid
> in three measures of meal, till the whole was leavened.
> —MATTHEW 13:33

God didn't call us to abandon society but to imbue it with the gospel. Jesus taught us here that His kingdom spreads progressively and gradually until the whole world is affected and hears the gospel!

As His salt and light, God is calling us to stop hiding ourselves and to infiltrate every level of life and society. He is holding our place in the world until we're ready to step in and take what is ours for His glory! Proverbs 13:22 says, "The wealth [all resources] of the sinner [wicked] is laid up [kept in store] for the just." Colossians 1:16 says, "All things were created by him, and *for him*" (emphasis added).

Sports stadiums were not built for half-drunken fans going wild over little balls going over big walls. God is saving them for our citywide prayer rallies. Imagine airplanes not only used by Christians to preach the gospel of the kingdom all over the world but saints actually owning whole airline companies. Perhaps there will be a company called Good News Airlines or Kingdom Carriers.

All the science, all the technology, all the life management strategies, all the money—all the resources of the world belong to God to be used for His glory! Why should Bill Gates and others be among the richest men in the world? Move over, Bill; in the future God is going to raise up apostles and prophets of technology who will use their talent and money for the kingdom. Why should Donald Trump and Leonna Helmsley own so much real estate? God is raising up Christian real estate moguls who will use their property to propagate and preach the gospel of the kingdom! (I am not saying that every Christian should be a billionaire. A lot of money would destroy certain believers. But I do believe God wants to prosper saints to the fullest extent of their spiritual and natural capabilities so that we can exert the most possible influence in our particular sphere.)

If the major reason why mosques can be built all over the world is because the rich oil reserves in Muslim countries finance their ministries, why shouldn't the church have access to the world's resources so the gospel can be financed? Someone might say, "God doesn't need our money." You ask any pastor what the biggest hindrance to vision is, and most will tell you it's finances! Any good leader knows that without money your vision will never manifest but will remain just an idea!

In the coming kingdom reformation one of the great signs of apostolic leadership will be the ability to access and connect with the right people for enormous amounts of resources. No longer will apostolic people just rely on tithes to finance the kingdom. No longer will they be known for just fundraising to build church buildings. Some Christian leaders will be involved in the exchanging of billions of dollars into the hands of the church. As apostolic leadership moves into the gospel of the kingdom of God, they will begin to use their apostolic anointing for creating and releasing finances on a scale never seen before!

They will walk in Deuteronomy 8:18 and 28:13; they will even lead the financial balance of resources from ungodly multinational corporations and banks into the hands of skilled Christian CEOs and entrepreneurs to pour into the body of Christ for community development and various kingdom ventures!

> But thou shalt remember the LORD thy God: for it is he that giveth thee power to get wealth, that he may establish his covenant which he sware unto thy fathers, as it is this day …And the LORD shall make thee the head, and not the tail; and thou shalt be above only, and thou shalt not be beneath; if that thou hearken unto the commandments of the LORD thy God, which I command thee this day, to observe and to do them.
> —DEUTERONOMY 8:18; 28:13

> And the children of Israel did according to the word of Moses; and they borrowed of the Egyptians jewels of silver, and jewels of gold, and raiment: And the LORD gave the people favor in the sight of the Egyptians, so that they lent unto them such things as they required. And they spoiled the Egyptians.
> —EXODUS 12:35–36

> A good man leaveth an inheritance to his children's children; and the wealth of the sinner is laid up for the just.
> —PROVERBS 13:22

Fivefold ministers will lead the way in kingdom economic sem-
inars and training, community development and education. There
will be hundreds of kingdom-based entrepreneurial magazines,
businesses, real estate and financial players. I believe that on the
other side of God's judgment, because of our country's semi-fascist,
semi-socialist philosophy of central control, government-directed
pagan public schools and forced redistribution by progressive
taxes, the church will soon be in a prime position to meet the needs
of the people! "Today in America, being an employee means you
are a 50/50 partner with the government. That means the government ultimately will take 50 percent or more of an employee's earn-
ing, and much of that before the employee sees the paycheck;"[8] on
the other hand, God only requires 10 percent. According to 1
Samuel 8:14–18, any civil government that extracts financially as
much as God requires is oppressive. Soon many civic and community leaders will look to churches, private industry and philan-
thropic societies to bail them out because they are finding that their
socialistic systems reek with failure!

Is the church ready for wholistic incarnational ministry? Are we
ready to go to the next level? If we are not willing to go to the next
level and network with the body of Christ to socially reconstruct
our cities…if we are not ready to go beyond talking and praying
about taking our cities…then the church in the next ten to twenty
years is going to miss out on its greatest opportunity for not only
keeping the harvest but mobilizing a harvest of souls that will
transform whole cities and nations!

CHAPTER 14

THE CONSEQUENCES OF THE KINGDOM

As we are wrapping up this book, I am going to use the last two chapters to briefly summarize most of the ideas that were brought forth. In this chapter I am going to repeat again some things that perhaps I only alluded to.

1. There will be a paradigm change.

Paradigm means the way you view something. Obviously I believe that the way leadership views the kingdom of God is going to drastically change. The biggest change, of course, will be that transition from just a platonic spiritual approach to a wholistic approach that permeates the whole natural world. The dichotomy between the "sacred" and the "secular" will end as the church realizes that "the earth is the Lord's and the fullness thereof."

2. There will be a leadership change.

In the coming kingdom reformation those leaders who don't want to make the paradigm change in their thinking and in their approach to ministry will struggle greatly or fail! The coming change will take place in the next ten to twenty years. The change will come because of the philosophy of the kingdom and the kind of wineskin God is building. Many true apostles will become elders in the gates of their nations and cities, and pastors will become the chaplains and spiritual leaders of their communities!

3. The body of Christ will embrace a wholistic vision.

In the next ten to twenty years it will be common for kingdom churches to include in their portfolio wholistic ministries such as job training, libraries, ministerial training centers, church-based theological training, learning centers, tutorial programs, family counseling, child placement services, maternity homes, homeless ministry, healthcare, credit unions and economic empowerment strategies.

The churches will not only teach people to give (something we're very good at now), but also to get, to buy, to manage and to invest!

4. Relocation

As the evangelical church grapples with and overcomes the sin of racism and desires to become that city on a hill, many saints will try to correct the sins of the fathers by moving their families back to the inner city. When saints begin to realize why they left the urban areas to begin with (since the 1920s the term became known as "white flight"), many will feel called of the Lord to work in the poorest neighborhoods of the cities and serve cutting-edge churches that are waging spiritual warfare and making a difference in their communities. We need to go beyond "Marching for Jesus." Some will be led to "move in for Jesus."

5. Partnerships

Most of the saints are not going to relocate to urban areas, but more and more of the evangelical churches in the suburbs and countryside will begin to partner with urban churches. When this kingdom paradigm shift takes place, pastors will not be able to rest until they begin to reach out beyond their local churches! Outer urban churches will begin to partner—not in a paternalistic way (that actually insults)—with urban churches as equals. Churches outside the city may have more financial resources, but they will begin to realize that they need the city church to teach them how to do effective wholistic ministry and intense spiritual warfare.

6. A change in secular society's leadership landscape

In the kingdom reformation, we will see more and more Christians infecting every level of society. Get used to seeing more and more real Christians in politics, Christians leading the way in finance, education, science and the arts! You will see more and more marketplace Christians speaking up and glorifying God! There will be more Christian-based media organizations like CBN and newspapers that will go beyond the ecclesiastical realm. (Move over, *Christian Science Monitor!*)

As spoken of earlier, there will be apostles and prophets of government, business, science, technology and the arts all making headline news. Instead of being relegated to the religious section of the newspapers, we will be dominating the front pages.

Many kingdom saints will even be the heads of cities and nations like Calvin and Abraham Kuyper (just as we see happening today in countries like Nigeria and Guatemala). As more and more

Christians with biblical world-views become high school teachers and college professors, look for the church to attract some of the greatest intellects in the world. Look for the creationism/evolution debate to get hotter and hotter with eventually creationism being taught once again in the public arena and in schools. As Christians flood the medical profession, look for abortions to continue to dissipate until it is again illegal! As more and more Christians move into secular news reporting, look for the anti-Christian media bias to begin to shift in the favor of the church. As whole communities are turned around by the apostolic kingdom strategies, look for more and more media focusing on the church for the answers we provide!

Many of the new waves of kingdom leadership are going to come from young people who live in poor neighborhoods. Some of our greatest intellects and civic leaders will originate from the poorest of areas that have previously been under the curse of poverty. These young ethnic people will rise up and stop "the desolations of many generations" and demonstrate that the gospel of the kingdom is not limited by environmental or psychological determinism but transcends all of societies' unfair presuppositions about so-called "minority peoples."

As you can see, my view of the future is glorious because as Isaiah 9:7 says, "Of the increase of his government and peace there shall be no end."

The influence of God's government on the earth is only going to get progressively greater, not diminish!

Hallelujah!

CHAPTER 15

COMMON MISCONCEPTIONS CLARIFIED

In closing out this book, I want to use this last chapter to briefly list some of the clarifications we've made about the gospel of the kingdom.

1.   Jesus is not just Lord of the church—He is Lord of the whole world.

And from Jesus Christ, who is the faithful witness, and the first begotten of the dead, and the prince of the kings of the earth. Unto him that loved us, and washed us from our sins in his own blood.

—REVELATION 1:5

And he hath on his vesture and on his thigh a name written, KING OF KINGS, AND LORD OF LORDS.

—REVELATION 19:16

All present leaders of the earth are required by God to submit to Him now—in this life! (This should motivate Christians to effect positive change in the social political arena.)

2.   Fivefold ministry is not only to be used in the church but also to infiltrate God's whole-created order.

He that descended is the same also that ascended up far above all heavens, that he *might fill all things*. And he gave some, apostles; and some, prophets; and some, evangelists; and some, pastors and teachers.

—EPHESIANS 4:10–11, EMPHASIS ADDED

3.   Being born again is to *see* the kingdom (to see the rule of God over all creation in this life), not just to go to heaven. John 3:3 says, "Jesus answered and said unto him, Verily, verily, I say unto thee, Except a man be born again, he cannot *see* the kingdom of God" (emphasis added).

4.   The church is not the kingdom of God—it is in the kingdom. The kingdom includes all of creation, not just the church.

5. Things are not predestined to get worse for the church. Matthew 16:18 says, "And I say also unto thee, That thou art Peter, and upon this rock I will build my church; and the gates of hell shall not prevail against it." (According to this verse and Revelation 2:5, the devil can't close churches. If a church shuts down, it's because God shut it down!)

6. God is not only interested in spiritual things. First Thessalonians 5:23 says, "And the very God of peace sanctify you wholly; and I pray God your whole spirit and soul and body be preserved blameless unto the coming of our Lord Jesus Christ." This verse clearly shows us God is concerned for the spiritual, mental and physical realm, not just the spiritual realm.

7. The purpose of revival is not just for souls to be saved, but also for societal reform to reflect heaven on earth. Matthew 6:10 says, "Thy kingdom come. Thy will be done in earth, as it is in heaven."

8. The Old Testament is important and should be seriously studied by Christians. The Old Testament is filled with hundreds of laws and principles dealing with civic government, finances, leadership management, education, family and sociology. It can be used as a guide to structure communities, cities and nations. When the early apostles preached, they only had the Old Testament for Scripture. Second Timothy 3:16 says, "All scripture is given by inspiration of God, and is profitable for doctrine, for reproof, for correction, for instruction in righteousness." When this verse was written, the full New Testament wasn't available; henceforth this verse was referring primarily to the Old Testament. (This should dispel the fallacious belief by some preachers that the Old Testament is only profitable for sermon illustrations!)

    You can't understand the New Testament without the Old Testament, and you can't understand the Old Testament (the shadow and type) without the illumination of the New Testament!

9. Political involvement is not unscriptural. (The Greek word for church, *ekklesia*, implies having strong civic leadership and participation.)

10. The gospel is not just for the poor, but also for the rich, the influential and for world leaders. (An earlier chapter showed how Paul the Apostle related to and reached the most influential people in a region.)

11. Redemption doesn't only affect the souls of men but also the whole created order. Colossians 1:20 says, "And, having made peace through the blood of his cross, by him to reconcile all things unto himself; by him, I say, whether they be things in earth, or things in heaven."

12. There is hope for inner cities. Isaiah 61:1, 4 says, "The Spirit of the Lord GOD is upon me; because the LORD hath anointed me to preach good tidings unto the meek; he hath anointed me to bind up the brokenhearted, to proclaim liberty to the captives, and the opening of the prison to them that are bound...And they shall build the old wastes, they shall raise up the former desolations, and they shall repair the waste cities, the desolations of many generations."

As you can see here, the purpose of God's anointing on the church is not just so that individuals can be restored, but also so that whole cities can be affected through the gospel of the kingdom. This coming kingdom reformation will also include urban centers and will get dramatic results. Jeremiah 29:7 tell us to seek the peace of the city. Let's obey this command.

Five years have passed since I wrote the manuscript for this book.

Before writing the book, I prophetically envisioned a major trend coming to the body of Christ at large that has now begun and is accelerating. After finishing the book in 1998, I experienced some frustration at not being able to interest a major Christian publishing company to publish the book. I felt the book could be a major contributor in terms of understanding the kingdom of God and the adjacent apostolic movement being manifest on earth. (To say the least I was very happy when Strang Communications contacted me and agreed to publish this work.)

The truths I shared in the book are even more relevant at this point in our nation's history than I ever dreamed because, in the post-9/11 climate, the world is depending more and more on the church even as elected officials are admitting their limitations, encouraging "faith-based" initiatives, and funneling state and federal funds to help subsidize holistic Christian community programs and ministries.

With the grave fiscal crisis hitting the nation and urban centers like New York City, many saints are panicking, complaining or planning on fleeing urban areas, but I believe that those seeing the needs of the people have the prescience to know that this can become the finest hour for the church!

Now, more than ever, the eyes of the world are upon us; they seem to be saying to us, "Put up or shut up!"

"Come on, let's see what you've got!"

"You have been saying to us for years that Jesus Christ has the answers for all of life; now show us if He can help us in our hour of need."

Truly, the world's moral, spiritual and financial bankruptcy is our chance to demonstrate to the cities and people of this nation that we not only have the answer for the next life, but for this life as well!

Instead of flaunting our "spirituality" and "mystically being content in blissful passivity," we should combine the work we do on our knees (prayer) with capable service to our fellow man, utilizing the intellectual, physical, and spiritual gifts and talents we as the church have been endowed with.

As social and cultural conditions in our nation rapidly deterio-
rate, the church has to seize the opportunity afforded us as soon as
possible!

It remains to be seen if the body of Christ is willing to lay aside
the old paradigm, "Being so heavenly minded means being no
earthly good," to obey the clear "cultural mandate" we have
received over and over again in both the Old and New Testaments.
(See Genesis 1:28 and Matthew 28:19.)

Sometimes it seems to me as though only a small remnant has
even begun to grasp the "gospel of the kingdom," and that most of
the church is still preoccupied with the rapture instead of obeying
the Lord's command, "Occupy until I come" (Luke 19:13, KJV).

In spite of all of this I have hope because throughout history the
church has experienced more challenging times than the present
and has come out triumphant!

I rest not in the ability of the saints in the church but in the ability of the God of the church to be sovereign and "rule...in the
midst of [His] enemies" (Psalm 110:2, KJV).

May the Lord breathe into this feeble attempt of mine to com-
municate biblical truth, and may He use it to continue the present
apostolic revolution in the church so society at large will be
"reformed" and more closely reflect God's ways so that "[His]
kingdom come, [His] will be done on earth as it is in heaven"
(Matt. 6:10).

—JOSEPH MATTERA

NOTES

INTRODUCTION
THE GOSPEL OF THE KINGDOM

1. More information and statistics can be found on the Bureau of Justice Statistics Crime and Justice Data Online website: www.ojp.usdoj.gov/bjs/.

CHAPTER 1
THE BIRTH OF THE PRAYER MOVEMENT

1. John Dawson, *Taking Our Cities for God*, rev. ed. (Lake Mary, FL: Charisma House, 1989, 2001).
2. Stephen R. Covey, *The 7 Habits of Highly Effective People* (New York: Simon and Schuster, 1990).

CHAPTER 6
WHY JESUS WAS CRUCIFIED

1. Francis A. Schaeffer, *How Should We Then Live?* (n.p.: Good News Publishers, 1983).

CHAPTER 10
THE NEXT MOVE: INCARNATION

1. Peter Marshall and David Manuel, *The Light And The Glory* (Old Tappan, NJ: Revell, 1980), 251–252.

CHAPTER 11
ARE YOU LIVING IN A GHETTO?

1. St. Augustine, *The City of God* (n.p.: Modern Library, 1994).
2. George Grant, *The Patriot's Handbook* (n.p.: Cumberland House, 1996), 93, 222.
3. Ray Bakke, *A Theology As Big As the City* (Downers Grove, IL: Intervarsity Press, 1997), 197–198.
4. Max Weber, *The Protestant Ethic and the Spirit of Capitalism*, second edition (n.p.: Routledge, 2001).
5. Donald Dayton, *Discovering an Evangelical Heritage* (Peabody, MA: Hendrickson Publishers, Inc., 1998).

CHAPTER 12
THE COMING APOSTOLIC REFORMATION

1. Mark Galli, "Tertullian: Pugnacious defender of faith," *Christian Reader* 39, No. 1 (January/February 2001): 15. Retrieved from the Internet at www.christianitytoday.com/cr/2001/001/12.15.html.
2. Ray Bakke, *A Theology As Big As the City*, 193.

CHAPTER 13
TEN THINGS ABOUT THE GOSPEL
OF THE KINGDOM

1. Francis A. Schaeffer, *A Christian Manifesto* (n.p.: Good News Publishers, 1982), chapter 1.
2. B. K. Kuiper, *The Church in History* (Grand Rapids, MI: Eerdmans, 1951), 174.
3. Ray Bakke, *A Biblical Word for an Urban World* (n.p.: Board of International Ministries of the American Baptist Churches, 2000), 1.
4. Henry Bettenson and Chris Maunder, eds., *Documents of the Christian Church* (New York: Oxford University Press, 1999), 164–181.
5. Bakke, *A Theology As Big As the City*, 12.
6. Ibid.
7. Ibid.
8. Robert T. Kiyosaki and Sharon L. Lechter, *Cashflow Quadrant: Rich Dad's Guide to Financial Freedom* (New York: Warner Books, Inc., 2000), 55.

Recommended Reading List

Bahnsen, Greg L. *Always Ready*. Texarkana, AR: Covenant Media Foundation, 1996. (Call 800-628-9460 to order.)

Bahnsen, Greg L. *Van Til's Apologetics*. Phillipsburg, NJ: Presbyterian and Reformed Publishing, 1998.

Barker, Joel Arthur. *Paradigms: The Business of Discovering the Future*. New York: Harper Business, 1993.

Belmonte, Kevin. *Hero for Humanity: A Biography of William Wilberforce*. Colorado Springs, CO: NavPress, 2002.

Breese, Dave. *Seven Men Who Rule the World From the Grave*. Chicago: Moody Press, 1990.

Chilton, David. *Productive Christians in an Age of Guilt Manipulators*. Tyler, TX: Institute for Christian Economics, 1985. (Call 800-628-9460 to order.)

Colson, Charles. *Developing a Christian Worldview of Science and Evolution*. Wheaton, IL: Tyndale, 2001. (Call 800-482-7836 to order.)

Colson, Charles and Pearcey, Nancy. *How Now Shall We Live?* Wheaton, IL: Tyndale, 1999.

Demar, Gary. *God and Government*. Powder Springs, GA: American Vision, 1990.

Dockery, David S. and Thornbury, Gregory Alan. *Shaping a Christian Worldview*. Nashville, TN: Broadman and Holman, 2002.

Johnson, Philip E. *Darwin on Trial*. Downers Grove, IL: InterVarsity Press, 1993.

Johnson, Phillip E. *The Case Against Naturalism in Science, Law, and Education*. Downers Grove, IL: InterVarsity Press, 1995.

Heslam, Peter S. *Creating a Christian Worldview*. Grand Rapids, MI: Eerdmans, 1998.

Juster, Daniel. *The Biblical Worldview*. San Francisco, CA: International Scholars, 1995.

Kuhn, Thomas. *The Structure of Scientific Revolutions*. Chicago, IL: University of Chicago Press, 1996.

Lewis, C. S. *Mere Christianity*. San Francisco, CA: Harper SanFrancisco, 2001.

Marsden, George. *The Soul of the American University: From Protestant Establishment to Established Nonbelief*. New York: Oxford University Press, 1994.

Naugle, David K. Worldview: *The History of a Concept*. Grand Rapids, MI: Eerdmans, 2002.

Noebel, David A. *Understanding the Times: The Religious Worldviews of Our Day and the Search for Truth*. Eugene, OR: Harvest House Publishers, 1991.

Peacocke, Dennis. *Doing Business God's Way*. Santa Rosa, CA: Rebuild Publishers, 1995. (Call 707-578-7700 to order.)

Peacocke, Dennis. *Winning the Battle for the Minds of Men*. Santa Rosa, CA: Strategic Christian Services, 1987. (Call 707-578-7700 to order.)

Rushdooney, Rousas. *The Philosophy of the Christian Curriculum*. Vallecito, CA: Ross House Books, 1985.

Schaeffer, Francis A. *A Christian Manifesto*. Westchester, IL: Crossway Books, 1981.

Schaeffer, Francis A. *The Great Evangelical Disaster*. Westchester, IL: Crossway Books, 1984.

Sowell, Thomas. *Basic Economics*. New York: Basic Books, 2000.

TO CONTACT THE AUTHOR

Write to: Pastor Joseph Mattera
Resurrection Church
740 40th Street
Brooklyn, NY 11232

Email: jmattera@resurrectionchurchofny.com

Phone: (718) 436-0242 ext. 15

Visit our Website at www.citycovenant.com.